HOW TO TURN YOUR COMPANY'S

PARABLES

INTO

PROFIT

A Business Is Known By The Stories It Tells

By: David Armstrong

How To Turn Your Company's Parables Into Profit

©   1995 by David M. Armstrong

Armstrong International, Inc.
2081 SE Ocean Boulevard - 4th floor
Stuart, FL 34997

ISBN 0-9648927-0-8

Printed in the United States of America

October, 1995

10 9 8 7 6 5 4 3 2 1

STORIES TO ENJOY

Special dedication

I dedicate this book to all the storytellers throughout the centuries. I start with the Master Himself, Jesus Christ, who told parables.

Special thanks to Aesop for his fables, Abraham Lincoln for his wonderful stories during troubled times, and Ronald Reagan, who loved telling stories.

Acknowledgements

I would like to thank Valerie Casterline and Patricia Powers for all their hard work and patience with me while writing this book. There is a part of Valerie and Patricia in each of these stories.

Special thanks to all the others who helped me put the stories together: David Casterline for helping to assure clarity of thought, Steve LaFalce for verifying grammar, Tom Morris who checked for legality as well as clarity of each story, and to all the people who the stories are about.

Foreword:
The Goose who Laid
the Golden Eggs

— Aesop, Greek Writer 620-560 B.C.

Early one morning a Farmer went to the nest of his Goose for an egg. When he looked inside the nest, he saw an egg that was like none he had ever laid eyes on before. It was shimmering gold. He picked it up. It was heavy. The egg was solid gold through and through.

"Wifey! Wifey!" he called. "Our Goosey has laid a golden egg for us!"

"Fancy that," said the Farmer's Wife. "Can I wear it around my neck?"

"You could, but your neck might break from the weight of it. It's solid gold!"

The Farmer's Wife felt how heavy the egg was and cried, "We're rich!"

Then the Farmer and his Wife joined hands and danced round and round the old kitchen table.

They did not have that old table for long. With the money they got from selling the egg, they went out and had an expensive new table made for themselves.

Each morning there was another golden egg waiting for them. And each day, the Farmer and his Wife sold the egg and bought something new.

One morning, the Farmer spotted the Goose as she was leaving her nest. Again, she had left him a glimmering gold egg. But the Farmer had become greedy and thought, "Why should I settle for just one egg each day? I'll open her up and take them all at once!"

So he chased his Goose round the farm until he caught her and killed her, and opened her up. But there were no eggs inside her. And now his good Goose was gone.

The Farmer stamped his feet and shook his fists to the sky for his foolishness. 🔥

Those who are too greedy end up with nothing.

The Parable of the Lost Son

— Jesus Christ

There was a man who had two sons. The younger one said to his father, "Father, give me my share of the estate." So he divided his property between them.

Not long after that, the younger son got together all he had, set off for a distant country and there squandered his wealth in wild living. After he had spent everything, there was a severe famine in that whole country, and he began to be in need. So he went and hired himself out to a citizen of that country, who sent him to his fields to feed pigs. He longed to fill his stomach with the pods that the pigs were eating, but no one gave him anything.

When he came to his senses, he said, "How many of my father's hired men have food to spare, and here I am starving to death! I will set out and go back to my father and say to him: Father, I have sinned against heaven and against you. I am no longer worthy to be called your son; make me like one of your hired men." So he got up and went to his father.

But while he was still a long way off, his father saw him and was filled with compassion for him; he ran to his son, threw his arms around him and kissed him.

The son said to him, "Father, I have sinned against heaven and against you. I am no longer worthy to be called your son."

But the father said to his servants, "Quick! Bring the best robe and put it on him. Put a ring on his finger and sandals on his feet. Bring the fattened calf and kill it. Let's have a feast and celebrate. For this son of mine was dead and is alive again; he was lost and is found." So they began to celebrate.

Meanwhile, the older son was in the field. When he came near the house, he heard music and dancing. So he called one of the servants and asked him what was going on. "Your brother has come," he replied, "and your father has killed the fattened calf because he has him back safe and sound."

The older brother became angry and refused to go in. So his father went and pleaded with him. But he answered his father, "Look! All these years I've been slaving for you and never disobeyed your orders. Yet you never gave me even a young goat so I could celebrate with my friends. But when this son of yours who has squandered your property with prostitutes comes home, you kill the fattened calf for him!"

"My son," the father said, "you are always with me, and everything I have is yours. But we had to celebrate and be glad, because this brother of yours was dead and is alive again; he was lost and is found."

With this story Jesus taught the people that
He had come not for those who thought they were good,
but for those who knew they had sinned.
God, our Father would always take us back—
no matter how bad our sins.

President Lincoln's Story

Abraham Lincoln once attempted to convince his Secretary of the Treasury, Salmon P. Chase, that it was a good idea for the government to issue interest-bearing currency as a means of raising money to support the war effort. Chase, however, objected to the proposal and argued that it was unconstitutional. Rather than simply ordering Chase to do it, which he could have as President, Lincoln chose to tell him a story.

An Italian captain ran his vessel on a rock and knocked a hole in her bottom. He set his men to pumping, and he went to pray before a figure of the Virgin in the bow of the ship. The leak gained on them. It looked at last as if the vessel would go down with all on board. The captain, at length, in a fit of rage at not having his prayers answered, seized the figure of the Virgin and threw it overboard. Suddenly the leak stopped, the water was pumped out, and the vessel got safely to port. When docked for repairs the statue of the Virgin Mary was found stuck, head foremost, in the hole.

Chase at first didn't see the precise application of the story. "Why, Chase," responded Lincoln, "I don't intend precisely to throw the Virgin Mary overboard, and by that I mean the Constitution, but I will stick it in the hole if I can. These rebels are violating the Constitution in order to destroy the Union; I will violate the Constitution, if necessary, to save the Union; and I suspect, Chase, that our Constitution is going to have a rough time of it before we get done with this row."

> *The spirit of the Constitution is more important than the written word.*
> —*David M. Armstrong*

Taken from *Lincoln on Leadership* by Donald T. Phillips, Warner Publishing Company. I would *highly* recommend you read this book.

The purpose of the Foreword is to convince you that storytelling has been around for centuries. Aesop's story is dated 620 B.C. The stories from Jesus are more than 2000 years old. President Abraham Lincoln's stories were told in the 1800s. These stories are still popular today. There is a good chance you knew the stories before you read them.

I believe storytelling is the most effective way to communicate, especially during these times of change... rapid change. We need a leadership tool, simple yet memorable, that will not change tomorrow. There are simply too many fads in how to become a successful leader today. Storytelling is timeless. It should come as no surprise that some of the greatest leaders loved to tell stories. Become a great leader...tell stories.

Happy Storying!
David

INTRODUCTION

The best introduction you had to storytelling could have been from your grandfather while you sat on his knee. Or maybe it was your mother who told you a story as you tried to fall asleep, or your father who told of his younger days. You've grown up with storytelling, but for some reason quit *believing* in it. Read this book and once again *believe* in the magic of storytelling. Storytelling is the best form of communication mankind has known and it can work in the business world, for any business.

The stories you are about to read have been written over a two-year period. A few of these stories may cover the same topic. That's okay. There is no doubt that one story will affect one person more than another. Why? If a person is familiar with the story it becomes more personal. This happens when someone has lived the story they are reading. The story's morals and quotes become more believable because the story is believable.

The morals can change with each story. The morals I wrote may not be the first ones that come to your mind. The morals I chose were what I wanted the story to focus on at that point in time. That's part of the magic of storytelling; you can pick the morals which highlight what you want to say.

Great companies take time to build. It has taken Armstrong International over 95 years to create its culture. Pick a *few* of your favorite stories and try to use them. Start slowly and keep it simple. If the results are good try a few more. The stories and their morals will only work if you really *believe* in what they say and give yourself time to make the changes. Aesop's fable, "Belling the Cat" maybe said it best in his moral,

"Some things are easier said than done."

Stories
that
kick start

urgency

1
The Day I Paid $248,000 to Play Golf

Come with me to the Sailfish Point Golf Course in sunny Florida. As I'm waiting to tee off on the first hole, I think to myself, "If my office needs me, they know I have my mobile phone." All day the phone never rings.

Upon my return to the office I find a phone message on my desk. It says,

"Please call Jerry Gilchrist."

As I dial the number I think to myself, "Good, somebody needs me."

"Hi, Jerry, I'm returning your call."

"Hi, David, I just bought two Computer Numeric Controlled (CNC) machines made by Wassino for $248,000."

I pause on the phone, "Jerry, what's the delivery time on these machines?"

"They're available within the week."

"Where are you going to find the room to put them?"

"We thought about scrapping or selling one of the single spindle machines and putting the two new machines around the Okuma CNC. That way, one man can run three machines at once."

"Will these machines run unmanned?"

"No, but we will get the machines next week which will help us with our current delivery problems. We can also use these machines on our new valve line."

"I remember last week we were talking about looking at used machines. Are these the used machines?"

"Yes. The reason we had to move so quickly to buy them was because another party was interested. Don Ely called me from the seller's location for a quick decision. He's checked the tolerances, maintenance, and hours operated on the CNC's. They have only been used six months. The machines look to be in great condition. Before I gave final approval to buy the machines, I talked to Steve Gibson and Ron Schlesch. With their positive comments and with the recommendation of Don Ely, I decided to buy the machines—even though it was over 12 times my spending authority."

"Jerry, I think you made a good decision."

> *Never put off 'til tomorrow what should be done today.*

THE MORAL OF THIS STORY

1. You never know when an urgent decision must be made.
If you're playing golf, sick, on vacation, in a meeting, or can't be found, who's going to make that decision? It doesn't matter if you're available, as long as the decision is made quickly.

2. Rules are meant to be broken given the right circumstances.
Jerry had a spending authority of $20,000 and he spent $248,000. He checked with Ron Schlesch, Steve Gibson and Don Ely before making his decision. Jerry was prepared to be held accountable. He felt comfortable in spending over 12 times his authorized limit without approval. Once you've carefully thought out your decision and checked with your experts, you must make the decision. Do your people feel this comfortable?

3. The questions leaders ask determines the attitude of their people. What was my first question? It was not, "Why did you spend $248,000 without my approval?" Questions like this create an environment of fear, distrust, and a lack of confidence.

4. $20,000 spending authority for an assistant general manager... Why so low if you really want to delegate authority? Remember, Jerry spent $248,000 — thus, it can be argued that he had no spending authority except the amount which he placed upon himself using common sense.

5. When delegating authority (and when it is PERCEIVED as truly being delegated) you accomplish three major goals: First, decisions are made more quickly; second, the people closest to the problem (who best know the solution) make the decision; third, you provide yourself with more time for other things — whether it be meetings, storytelling, acquisitions, coaching, training or even playing golf.

2
✔

The new week began as people arrived at work. As they approached their work stations, each noticed a calendar strategically located where it would be easily seen. On the calendar was a blue check mark with no explanation.

Curiosity set in.

The next week, posters arrived in the plant with a blue check mark—creating yet more curiosity. Soon, the staff found coffee mugs, hats, scratch pads, parking places, and other items with blue check marks on them. This was a mystery which had to be solved!

Finally, they were told what the blue check mark stood for: "Consider it Done."

"Consider it Done" is the new vision statement for Armstrong International, Inc. and all its divisions. The blue check mark is a symbol which we use to "check" off items on a list of things to do.

The new vision statement promotes urgency in every decision made at Armstrong. Since this philosophy of urgency had been promoted for the past two years through the old vision statement, "Armstrong—Expect a Difference Now," it was essential to build excitement and interest in the new vision statement. It was critical to use curiosity and mystery while promoting it. 🔥

Today, the tortoise would lose the race to the hare.

THE MORAL OF THIS STORY

1. Remember the childhood story about the race between the tortoise and the hare? Steady and sure toward your goal was the moral of the story. As my quote reveals, today you cannot just be steady and sure and expect to win! Too many competitors (hares) are moving fast and one of those hares won't fall asleep.

2. "Consider it Done"—our vision statement: Whatever you are working on, do it quickly and stay within the boundaries of your corporate core values. When faced with a question of what to do, the answer will come more easily if you remember to practice urgency.

3. "Consider it Done" is for everyone. Clearly, the success of our vision will depend upon continuous use and reinforcement at all levels in our company. This vision statement applies to all.

4. "Consider it Done" can work for every division. Your division may have its own strategy or business plan that promotes service, quality, innovation, etc. Corporate's vision also should be applied to your strategy. If you're focusing on quality, you should do so quickly. If it's innovation, be the fastest at developing new products.

5. Like storytelling, urgency is here to stay! Our society and technology are changing rapidly. In the past, product improvement took years; today it takes months; tomorrow it will take days. Today's emphasis on quality, service, innovation, diversification, acquisition, downsizing, or whatever, will pass with other fads. Urgency, on the other hand, will always be needed to implement the newest fad into our business before our competitors do. Our vision—can last forever!

6. Do your words and actions promote urgency? If asked, "Can my order ship today?"—"Can you finish it today?"—"When can you repair the machine?"—"Can you call this customer back?"—Your answer, **"Consider it Done."**

3
Fits of Urgency

Wal-Mart and Armstrong International, Inc. have something in common: both are masters of "fit." Tom Peters uses the word "fit" when he describes Wal-Mart's drab, two-story building (with Formica desks and battleship-gray walls) and founder Sam Walton's small office. Wal-Mart competes by using the strategy of everyday low prices. They have made sure that they fit this strategy. By putting Wal-Mart's dollars into operations instead of corporate furnishings they have captured the market where low prices prevail. "It's difficult to live a fast-paced, bare-boned, discount strategy if you live in ponderous surroundings," says Tom.

Armstrong is a master of fit when it comes to urgency. Hard things, such as mobile phones, fax machines, large inventory and a flexible machining system (FMS), are all "fits" of urgency. We also don't forget the soft things, such as returning a customer's call the same day... even better, within the hour... better yet, by answering the phone within three rings. Delegation of authority is a sure method of promoting urgency because people are thereby empowered to act. The celebration of past failures, promotions for cheaters of bureaucracy, and establishment of self-management teams are also evidence of urgency. Recognition plaques, stories and bonus programs supporting urgency all help Armstrong obtain the title of "Master of Fit of Urgency."

> *"If you're considering change, first consider fit."*
> —*Tom Peters, Business Writer*

THE MORAL OF THIS STORY

1. Becoming a master of fit is accomplished through both of what I call hard and soft methods. I believe you need both to be successful. One cannot expect urgency simply because you have a fax machine (hard). You must also pick up and route the faxes quickly (soft). Letting a fax remain in the machine does not "fit" urgency.

2. Your vision statement must agree with your fit. It must be crystal clear to all your employees that your "fit" matches your vision statement. If not, you may confuse them. Our vision statement, "Consider it Done," does "fit" the way we live at Armstrong.

3. Invest in your fit. Your employees and leaders will feel compelled to practice your fit if you have invested in it. At Armstrong, we've invested money in fax machines, a flexible machining system, CAD systems, large inventory, bonus programs and training by satellite, all of which promote urgency.

4. If you want to fit, be where the action is. Armstrong's executives and leaders are willing to leave their offices and visit the factories because that's where urgency is practiced. It's not in their offices. If you want to win the game of urgency, you have to go to the playing field.

5. If you want to fit, go where the action takes you. Armstrong's workers must also be willing to leave their machines or work stations and visit the offices of the leaders if they need a quick decision. Waiting for your leader to come and help you is not urgent enough.

4
A Wooden 2" x 4"

Armstrong-Hunt, Inc., Florida has always had a problem finding enough floor space for inventory. As most plants have done in this situation, they decided to stack their inventory on shelves. The big fear with stacking inventory on shelves is a safety problem. You never know when a rack may collapse or something might fall off the top shelf.

One day Chuck Herlehy, who is a sheet metal worker, cornered Chuck Rockwell in the Armstrong-Hunt plant. His concern was that a rack in his department (which held tube supports) was being used improperly. On the top shelf a wooden 2" x 4" had been positioned to help extend the arms so that more stock could be stored on the shelf. The tube supports had fallen off the shelf in the past due to this unsafe stacking procedure.

Herlehy's fear was that somebody would eventually get hurt. Chuck Rockwell, the general foreman, decided to delegate the responsibility of correcting the problem to Chuck Herlehy. Within hours he had relocated all the tube supports to ground level. He also removed the 2" x 4" which had been used improperly.

> *Practice our Core Values; Safety, Honesty, Loyalty—*
> *Is it legal, moral and fair?*

THE MORAL OF THIS STORY

1. Create an atmosphere that encourages taking spontaneous initiative. How do you do that? By destroying all unnecessary layers of command—to help speed up decision making. Due to the fact that Chuck Rockwell delegated the responsibility the problem was put into the proper hands. Get your people to do something. Here, we find Chuck Herlehy taking it upon himself to fix a problem dealing with safety. I believe there are few people in our company that would walk away from a safety problem without fixing it. Now, ask yourself the same question when dealing with quality, service or innovation. Would you do something in these areas, or would you walk away?

2. Nothing has a higher priority than a core value. Chuck Herlehy supported one of our core values—safety. He did this within hours. One test to find out if your people support your core values is to look for quick action being taken to solve or avoid a problem involving a core value.

3. Always listen to your people. You never know when they are going to have something to tell you which will benefit the company. Here, we see Chuck Rockwell taking the time to listen to Chuck Herlehy regarding a safety problem.

5
P-E-R-F-E-C-T-I-O-N-I-S-M

It was early morning when I arrived in the Punch Press Department at Armstrong International, Inc., Michigan. Bill Hartman, department foreman, was on the phone so I took a seat and waited. I looked over at the 250-ton punch press and noticed that it was stamping production. Bill hung up the phone.

"So, David, what can I do for you today?"

"Well, Bill, I'm curious. Does the punch press have the safety features on it that I asked for?"

Bill drops his head and with a very soft answer says—"No."

"I don't understand. I asked more than three months ago for safety devices to be put on. You remember! We talked about installing magnetic fields or sensor pads on the floor, so if someone got too close to the machine, it would turn off."

Bill answered, "That was the last I heard two months ago, and I haven't heard anything since. All I know is they're working on it."

"What else in this department is not safe?"

Bill thinks for a moment, "We have a portable table on wheels that we use for moving 700-pound dies from racks to machines."

"So what's the problem with the table?"

"Well, we adjust it to the height of the rack where the dies are stored, then we slide the dies on the table. We then wheel it over to the machine. The problem is the table is too wide for the machine so we have to angle it in toward the machine. As we slide the die off there's an open space since only a corner of the table is lined up with the machine."

"So what can happen?" I interrupt.

"It's already happened. We've actually dropped 700-pound dies on the floor, and I've told my guys to be careful because their steel toe shoes aren't going to make any difference when 700 pounds hits them."

"How long has this been going on?"

"Oh, we've had this table since the 1970s."

I couldn't believe what I was hearing.

"Bill, have you talked to anybody about it?"

"Yes, I put it into the capital budget but I haven't heard anything in the last eight months. Nobody seems to know if it was approved."

"Bill, I'm here to tell you I never saw it on the capital budget, so it's not approved. What are you going to do about it?"

"Well, I guess I'll wait and see if they get back to me with a solution."

"Bill, I can't believe I'm hearing this! You of all people know how important safety is. You're the foreman of this department. I know you're not afraid to be heard. You are one of our best employees. If anybody is sure of himself, it's you, and yet even you won't speak up and and get this done! Make a fuss, Bill, get it done."

I leave Bill Hartman and work my way toward the strainer department where I find Jack Vanscoik.

"Jack, three months ago you told me about a safety concern. We talked about you getting some type of hoist to lift the heavy strainers because of your back problems. Has that been taken care of?"

"No, David, I haven't heard anything."

"You haven't?" I ask.

"Nope."

"I'm sorry, Jack. I'll look into it."

I walked over and talked to Danny Bronstetter, the foreman of the assembly department.

Dan said, "Manufacture Engineering is working on the problem, but the original estimates were over $20,000.00. They hope there is a cheaper and better way to do it. They just haven't figured it out yet. In the meantime, I have people available to help Jack lift the strainers, and he's been told not to lift them by himself."

"That's all good, Dan, but Jack brought this to our attention over nine months ago and we still haven't fixed it."

A special foremen's meeting was called that morning by Rex Cheskaty, general manager, and me. This is what we decided:

Time flies when using perfection.

THE MORAL OF THIS STORY

1. Safety gets a high priority in capital budgets. If unreasonable safety problems occur which can be corrected, we will deal with them quickly. There will be no delays for correctable safety problems due to lack of funds in the capital budget. We will add the funds.

2. P-e-r-f-e-c-t-i-o-n-i-s-m results in unnecessary delays. Trying to find the perfect solution results in delays. During this time accidents can occur. I believe it is better to solve the problem 80% and do it now and protect the people now. Attempting to fix safety problems with p-e-r-f-e-c-t-i-o-n-i-s-m was the reason for the delays with the 250-ton punch press and Jack's hoist for heavy strainers.

3. Use outside contractors when you're too busy. We cannot do everything or be the best at everything. Sometimes it is faster and cheaper to contract the job outside our company. Originally the maintenance department was going to cut four inches off the table so it would better fit our machines. The cost to do this would have been high and the time to do it would have caused long delays due to the heavy schedule in the maintenance department. To save time, we talked about sending the table out to be fixed, but in the end, we purchased a new table that very next day.

4. A capital request deserves an answer... yes or no. Management must take an answer back to the person who made the request.

Don't forget to tell them why the decision was made, and if it will be implemented—when.

5. The price of safety is your responsibility. You know if it's not safe. You don't need someone to tell you. You manage your own tardiness (no time clocks), your own money (open coin box in cafeteria), your own quality (self inspection), so it's up to you to take responsibility for safety and not blame it on management. It's just as much your fault as management's if unsafe conditions exist.

Stories
to make
people
brave and wise

CHAPTER II

6
Exposed in the Men's Room

"I wonder what time it is? Hum, 2:00 p.m. I'll bet I could be in Atlanta by 7:00 tonight, stay with my friends and be home by tomorrow afternoon. I wonder where the Florida turnpike is? There it is!"

Several hours pass. "How much gas do I have? An eighth of a tank...hmm, almost empty. I think I'll pull into the next gas station."

"That will be $20.00, sir."

"Can I have a receipt, please? Thanks."

As Hazen Kreis III walks to his car, he sees four bass boats lined up at the gas pumps. Hazen, district sales manager for Computrol, Idaho, approaches each of the boat owners and hands them literature.

"I'm not trying to sell you anything today. I'm a factory representative and I think you will find this literature interesting. While you're on the road, have someone in the car read it to you. You'll enjoy the story about the Bottom Line fish finders." Hazen waves goodbye as he leaves in his car.

Two hours later..."Boy, I'm getting thirsty. I think I'll pull into the next rest area. I'll take a large Coke, please. Thank you."

As Hazen walks out, the four fishermen he had met earlier ran up to him.

"We've been following you for two hours. We couldn't catch you."

"I was only going 67 mph." "We know, but we can only go 65 mph while pulling our boats. We want one of those fish finders."

"Here's a list of local distributors in your area. I think you'll be…"

"No, wait, you don't understand. We want one NOW!"

"Gentlemen, I don't have any to give you right now. All I've got is a demo unit and I'm not allowed to sell it. Tell you what I'll do. I'll take you in and give you a live demonstration on how it works."

They walk back into the rest stop area looking for an electrical outlet to plug the unit into. Finally their search leads them into the men's restroom.

"BEEP...there's a fish at 28 feet. BEEP… there's a fish at 46 feet off the starboard," explains Hazen.

Other men in the restroom become interested and want to know what's going on. A few minutes passed, "There you have it… the Bottom Line **Sidefinder**.

"Where can we get one this week?" asked one of the boaters.

"Just go to any of the big retail shops, such as Kmart, Wal-Mart, Bass Pro Shops, Sports Authority, Sports Unlimited, etc., and they'll have a unit you can purchase."

When Hazen gets home, he calls his boss and tells him what happened. His boss says with a chuckle, "You know, Hazen, you shouldn't expose the company in the men's room like that."

Timing is everything.

THE MORAL OF THIS STORY

1. Hazen knew the time was now… if he wanted to reassure the fishermen to buy a Bottom Line **Sidefinder** (fish finder). Sometimes the place is not as important as the time. How many approvals have you received in the hallway, by your car or even at coffee break?

2. When making a capital request, consider the timing...is it good or bad? If there's a recession, cash flow is tight, or the company just purchased several machines, your timing is probably bad.

3. When giving someone a raise, promotion, termination notice, or demotion, consider the timing. When giving someone their walking papers, you don't do it before a holiday. Most of us know this. Are you careful when you're giving a promotion or raise? We get so few opportunities to be the bearer of good news. Make the most of it. Remember your timing!

4. If you need approval for an idea, wait for the right moment. Don't rush it and lose the order. You'll know when the time is right.

7
It Rained Cats and Dogs

That's what it did last night, it rained cats and dogs.

As the rain filled the streets and the drains began to fill, the water started creeping over the street curb. The water worked its way up the sidewalk and arrived at the doorsteps of Armstrong International, Inc., Michigan. The rain soon passed beneath the door, entered through our lobby (Home Sweet Home) and began to seep through the ceiling of the basement and pour down the stairs. The basement is where we keep all the transfer stations for our phone system. It was also the temporary home for the brand new Computer Aided Design (CAD) system that we had just purchased. We were holding training sessions, and the CAD system was in a room downstairs, with a processor for each station on the floor.

That same morning, David Pinkerton and Danny Blasius were awakened by their alarm clocks. They had agreed to meet at 4:00 a.m. at Armstrong to do a special electrical job. By doing this job before office hours they could avoid the inconvenience of shutting down the computers, telephones and other electrical equipment during working hours.

You can imagine David and Danny's surprise when they found themselves face to face with an actual stream of water running down the hallway and into the basement! Quickly, they went downstairs, picked up all the CAD equipment off the floor and put it on tables. They also took plastic and covered the CAD system and as much of the phone equipment as possible. They did their best to prevent more water from coming in and began mopping up the water. David and Danny's quick actions saved the CAD system and most of our phone system; maybe they saved the company from shutting down for the day. 🔥

> *The harder you work, the luckier you get.*
> *— Gary Player, golf professional*

THE MORAL OF THIS STORY

1. Success depends on being in the right place at the right time. This is true, but it also helps to work hard. The harder you work, the more opportunities you'll have to be successful, to be noticed. David and Danny's going to work at 4:00 a.m. is definitely a sign of working hard. By working hard they had an opportunity to save the day. Don't wait for your opportunities; make your opportunities happen by working hard!

2. When you see your opportunity, you must take action. David and Danny saw a problem, took action and saved valuable equipment. I am convinced that many people have opportunities in their lifetime and either don't recognize them, are afraid to take a chance, or don't act quickly enough, thereby missing their chance to become more successful.

3. Ability is nothing without opportunity. David and Danny both have ability, but they needed an opportunity to show what they could do. Several leaders, including myself, heard about this story. That's great exposure for David and Danny! It's great when the boss hears about or sees you doing something that benefits the company. And don't think we forgot it was 4:00 a.m.!

L. CONRAD

8
My First Lesson in Motivation

Summer vacation had just begun. I was only 18 years old. I had my first job working in the shop at Armstrong International, Inc., Michigan. I was assigned to the machining department. I worked on several machines so I could learn the function of each machine and get to know the people who ran them. I remember getting my first lesson on what motivates people.

"Good morning, David. Let's get started," said Fred.

"This work order tells us what to machine and how many parts to run. Let's see…we have to run five hundred 211 caps. The first thing we do is find the fixture which holds the 211 cap and put it on the drill press."

A few minutes pass, "Now what do we do?" I ask.

Fred responds, "Now we pick the correct size drill bit and put it into this jig which goes on the machine. Then we set the machine at the proper speed. Now we can start drilling the holes."

One hour passes, two hours pass and I still have not drilled a hole, but I'm watching Fred pull the handle down as he finishes one cap after another. I'm thinking to myself, "I'm not sure I could do this for the rest of my life."

"Fred, how long have you been doing this job?"

"Let's see, 20 years come June."

"**Twenty years** doing the same job?" I repeated.

"Yeah… 20 years."

The foreman of the shop comes up and interrupts our conversation.

"Excuse me, Fred, you remember Bill who retired last week?"

"Yes, he was a good man."

"We would like to offer you his job. It will require learning a new job. It's a little more complex, but we know you can do it."

Fred stops pulling the handle and says, "You can't make me work on Bill's machine. I won't do it. I'll quit first. I like this job."

The foreman, startled and confused, says, "It's okay, Fred. You can continue doing this job. We just thought you'd like a change."

"No, I like what I'm doing."

The day ended and I found myself going home confused.

To each his own.

THE MORAL OF THIS STORY

1. We are all different in our desires and wants… and it's a good thing we are. Fred enjoyed doing what he did, but I couldn't understand why. How could anyone do the same job for 20 years and be content, motivated, fulfilled and not bored? Then my father explained, "David, be happy there are people in this world who enjoy doing what Fred does. Don't assume just because you wouldn't be happy and content that Fred wouldn't, either. He's not you."

2. Leading people is difficult and now you know why. Everyone is different. Understanding how people feel and what motivates them is not easy. We as leaders are not here to **judge** the way others find fulfillment in their lives. That's their decision with God. We, as leaders, are here to understand the **dreams** of our people and try to make them come true.

9
A Temper Tantrum

Long ago, we had a shop superintendent named Leu. Leu had a man working for him named Bob. Bob received *glowing* reviews on his work performance every year. There was never a problem; in fact, he was considered a *good* worker!

Now it came to pass that Leu was having a terrible day when Bob crossed his path. One thing led to another and before Leu knew it, he lost his temper and fired Bob. Word traveled fast (as bad news always does), and soon the founder of the company, Adam Armstrong, overheard what had happened.

Adam approached Leu and reviewed all the facts and details. Leu admitted that he had lost his temper, and that Bob had been given good reviews in the past and had never been a problem. At that point, Adam realized what had to be done.

Adam said, "Leu, I want you to rehire Bob and do it now!"

> *Your temper is one of your more valuable possessions.*
> *Don't lose it.*

THE MORAL OF THIS STORY

1. Temper gets you into trouble, pride keeps you there. If you are angry, wait one day before making your decision or saying something. If you see somebody getting angry with you, offer to discuss it the next day.

2. We don't get angry with customers, so don't get angry with the employees.

3. To benefit from the strengths of leaders, we must tolerate some of their weaknesses.

4. A leader with anger scares people. If you don't control your anger, people will hide their problems and real thoughts from you. They will avoid you!

5. Think before you speak. You will be much further ahead in the long run, and people will respect you for your patience.

Stories
to turn
us into
change gourmets

CHAPTER III

10

In the year 1042, a fierce battle was taking place when the King of Scotland fell from his horse. Before the King could be killed, a man named Siward Beorn jumped from his horse and picked up the fallen King by his royal leg, armor and all, and using only *one* arm hoisted him up into the saddle. When the battle was over, the King of Scotland summoned the man who had saved his life: "Bring me the one who lifted me with one strong arm into his horse's saddle."

When Beorn came before the king, he knelt and the King said, "For your startling feat of strength, I hereby dub you 'the strong arm'." Over a period of generations, this name changed to Armstrong. The King also gave Armstrong a family crest which he described as "an armed hand and arm; in the hand a leg and foot in armor, cut at the thigh. This crest is to symbolize you picking up your fallen King by my royal leg, and using only one hand to hoist me up into the saddle."

Adam Armstrong, founder of our company, also remembered this story. When Armstrong International, Inc., Michigan designed the first Inverted Bucket Steam Trap in 1910, you can guess what the logo of the company was; he used a picture of a muscular arm holding a steam trap in the air. During the early years,

Armstrong held the lion's share of the steam trap market; that is, until the 1950s when the disc trap was invented by competition. Through the next two decades, Armstrong's market share fell.

A new war was upon us in the 1970s; the war of energy conservation. Since Armstrong's Inverted Bucket Steam Trap lasted longer than other generic traps, it became the best energy saver. Armstrong's position on the war of saving energy had to be made clearer. We decided to change our logo to the letter "A" with a sun full of energy bursting through the center of the "A." Armstrong regained its status as the "number one" manufacturer of steam traps in the United States because our Inverted Bucket Steam Trap saved energy.

The 1990s brought on a new war; a war to protect the environment. Since Armstrong's Inverted Bucket Steam Traps have the longest service life, they waste less energy which means you burn less fuel and reduce emissions. And that makes for a cleaner, healthier environment. Armstrong Steam Traps are helping to protect the world we all share. May our company logo reveal the side that we take; protecting the environment and saving energy.

THE MORAL OF THIS STORY

1. Company logos can outlive people and products; even the buildings on which they hang. Company logos die only when major change is required or from lack of use. Promote the use of your logo through advertising. Put your logo on envelopes, letterhead, purchase orders, payroll checks, scratch pads, whatever you can find. Help keep it alive!

2. One of your company's most important assets is its logo. Protect it by keeping it alive as I mention above. It will help make us more money since it builds loyalty with our customers.

3. Did you forget your products? Do they have your company's name and logo on them? They should, and it should be attached so it won't come off. It's just as important as those product features you promote. Be careful though, of line extension. An example of line extension is if Life Savers (candy) used the brand name Life Savers for a new product (gum). Would you buy gum because it says Life Savers? Of course not. The corporate logo and name won't sell everything, so *don't* put it on all our new products. Use brand names with our company logo, for example, Armstrong's **Flo-Rite-Temp.**

VI ET ARMIS

11
A Barrel of Apples

There was a time when wooden barrels were used to hold water, gunpowder, salt and sugar. The barrel was also seen in corner stores where it held apples.

As time went on the barrel became outdated. Thus, the barrel was put into storage. During this storage period, the barrel began to think of other ways to become useful to mankind. "In the year 2000 mankind will want to simplify inventory control. What could be easier than looking into me and making sure I'm filled to the top? No college degree, no experience required, just the ability to see, write out the order, and walk to the next barrel." The barrel smiled with relief as it rolled over. "In the future, they will need me to help control inventory. I'll be back!"

The year 2000 is coming sooner than you think. Just wait, the barrel will become a part of our life again! The barrel will evolve from the general store to factories. We will find barrels in every department and next to every machine. The barrels will contain parts for products. Someone will walk through the factory every day and look into each barrel. If the barrels are not full, work orders will be generated to fill them.

This story sounds ridiculous, maybe even like science fiction, but it is not. It's a true story. In the 1950s, Armstrong International, Inc., Michigan used barrels to control inventory as many companies did. Claire Kaiser, shop superintendent at that time, would walk through the plant (MBWA as we know it today) and inspect the barrels. If he found a barrel half-full, he might tell the machinist to fill it to the top. He would then walk to the next barrel and if it was a quarter full, he might insist the barrel be filled half-way. Unfortunately for the barrel, the computer age was around the corner.

When we bought our first mainframe computer, we gradually stopped using the barrel and started using monthly average usages, safety stock and reorder points to control inventory. We took a simple procedure and complicated it, but our payback was improvement in inventory control (more accuracy), thereby improving customer service by having the parts required to fill the orders. 🔥

> *Some men see things as they are and say, "WHY?"*
> *I dream of things that never were and say, "WHY NOT?"*
> *— George Bernard Shaw, author*

THE MORAL OF THIS STORY

1. Today a brilliant idea, tomorrow a silly idea. Remember when the story revealed that in the year 2000 barrels were going to be used to control inventory? Remember how you thought it was a silly idea and would never happen? Then the story ends and you find that we had already used barrels in the 1950s to control our inventory. Crazy ideas can work, so keep an open mind.

2. Why not use barrels to control inventory... and later change to computers for inventory control? One day we will have MRP-II, Kanban, or a flow process to replace our current inventory system. The point is, we should not be afraid to change, even if the change sounds like something out of science fiction.

3. "In the beginner's mind, there are many possibilities, but in the expert's there are few." Shunryu Suzuki, who wrote this, would clearly understand the barrel story. Our experts overcomplicate things and forget that simplicity still works. Think as a child does, who believes in science fiction.

12
Flash Gordon Would be Proud of Barb Gordon

"Hi, Barb! I thought I'd come out to the shop and see how things are going with your new job. When did you transfer from the office to the shop?"

"Oh, about three weeks ago."

"Is everybody treating you fairly and being nice?"

"Yes, everyone has been real kind and helpful."

"Barb, what job do they have you doing?"

"I'm assembling EHU subassemblies."

"Oh, I remember doing that. That was one of my favorite jobs when I worked in the shop."

"Yes, it sure makes the day go by fast. When I worked in the office, I'd watch the clock because the days went by so slowly. That's why I asked you and Jerry if I could move out to the shop."

"I remember when you offered to work in the shop half-days because you wanted to give it a try. Was it as bad as you thought?"

"No — I was a little scared at first and didn't know what to expect, but now I really enjoy it here. As a matter of fact, I was wondering if I could move to the shop full-time? I know they can keep up in the office by reallocating my workload to others. I'd still like to work with the college help this summer and then go full-time when they leave."

"Sure, Barb, I think we can move you to full-time in the shop. We'll look at it in a month or two. 🔥

> *It's easier to make changes when your company is in trouble—and not so easy when you're doing well.*

THE MORAL OF THIS STORY

1. Barb, if I had a medal to pin on you I would... better yet, I'll write a story about you. It's easy for people to perform heroic deeds and for companies to have major turnarounds when their jobs are in jeopardy or the company is about to go out of business. During good times, people seldom sacrifice their comfort zone and offer to do something exceptional for the company. Armstrong International, Inc., Michigan and Barb were not in trouble. Barb Gordon, however, left a "comfortable" office because she could be more productive in the shop. She wanted to work, not watch the clock tick.

2. Fear of the unknown is sometimes the worst fear of all. Barb was unsure whether she wanted to go to the shop so she offered to go half-time. After being on the job only three weeks, she asked if she could become full-time in the shop. Sometimes we find ourselves in situations where we can make decisions or try something new, but those inner fears take over and tell us to play it safe. Few people get ahead in this life by "playing it safe." The *key* is to find people who exhibit risk-taking traits and have the inner drive and motivation to *help*. How will Barb get ahead? She will enjoy her work more, the days will go by faster and she will position herself to be more valuable to the company. Don't think that we fail to notice people who are not busy.

3. Do more with less... Expense reductions, personnel reductions, plant closings, inventory reductions, etc., are only part of the answer. All companies, no matter how successful, go through periods where they must clean house and reduce their waste. Cutting expenses helps, but so does doing more with what is left.

4. The office is more difficult to run lean than the shop. Why? Because building a product is an easy thing to measure; you can count the units. You know if you need more help and on what machines. How do you measure the value of reports, service calls, engineers' time, or the leader's value in setting goals, making decisions, reviewing status reports, etc.? Soft stuff is hard to measure, and if it's hard to measure, it's difficult to know where to stay lean.

13
Lights, Camera, Action!

In 1972, long before Blockbuster Video was a household word, Carolyn Roberts, director of corporate marketing services, Armstrong International, Inc., Michigan, developed a complete library of educational videotapes, handbooks and other materials to train our customers on the use of our products. The initial customer reaction was exciting! Next, she asked our representatives to distribute the tapes and handbooks to our customers.

We sell and service our products by a network of independent sales representatives. Carolyn naturally assumed that the representatives would be excited with the prospect of being able to solve their customers' need for education in product usage. Imagine Carolyn's surprise when the representatives' attitude was negative! She had the serious problem of trying to find a way to motivate our representatives to distribute our training materials. She hired a communications consultant to help. After listening to Carolyn's story, the consultant asked: (1) Are your representatives *capable* of carrying out your request? (Have *they* received the proper training?); and, (2) Have *you* provided them with the necessary tools to carry out your request?

Carolyn discovered she had *not* clearly thought out the problems the representatives would encounter. With their needs in mind, she developed an innovative new direct marketing binder, including a training aids brochure and a preview videotape called "Hot Clips," which explained our complete training program. When presented with these new tools, our representatives enthusiastically began presenting our training materials to the customers.

By taking the time to listen to the reasons for our representatives' negative attitude, we were able to develop the tools they needed. The result has benefited our customers, our representatives and Armstrong. 🔥

> *Tis harder to "unlearn" than learn.*
> — *Barber, Book of 1000 Proverbs*

THE MORAL OF THIS STORY

1. The biggest cost in training may be time. If you encounter a negative attitude from someone you have asked to carry out a request, it's quite possible *you* have not done your homework. Take time to consider: (1) Is the person capable of carrying out your request (i.e., do they have the necessary training)?; (2) Do they have the necessary tools?; and, (3) Have you clearly thought through all the problems the person will encounter?

2. What is popular isn't always right, and what is right isn't always popular. When Carolyn first used videotapes to train our customers on the use of our products, it was not popular with our representatives. They were still using literature and personal sales calls. Videotapes were too impersonal, expensive and, let's be honest, different! Time proved all these assumptions to be wrong. Our videotapes helped us gain market share and our customers and representatives became comfortable with them to the point where, over the years, we have generated over 15 teaching videos.

3. "Knowledge must be invited in." Dr. Deming was right when he said this! If your representatives don't want to learn, there is very little you can do to train and teach them. You must first get their attention with something new and different. A videotape was different.

4. We have invested in Carolyn's idea. We have invested over $1.5 million in our videotape library. We wouldn't invest that kind of money if it weren't a good idea.

Stories to get people to *communicate* about things worth *communicating* about

14
Shoe Box

David Nelson, Jr. was working in the assembly department at Everlasting Valve Corporation, New Jersey, when I first met him. He is a big man with a beard and his hands are often dirty from working on the valves. But every time I talk to him, a smile appears on his face. This day was no exception.

"Hi, David," I said. "Do you have any stories for me today?"

"No, I can't think of any."

"Have you done anything to improve our urgency?"

"No, I can't think of anything right offhand."

Just then, Rodney Belle, who also works in assembly, waved at me.

"How's it going, Rodney?"

"Fine, Dave."

"Rodney, can you come here for a minute? Why don't you and David follow me and we'll look at the stories on the bulletin board?"

While walking to the bulletin board, we talked about why stories are important. Sure enough, the stories were located on the bulletin board for everyone to read. "Guys, help me remind the others where the stories can be found. If everyone reads them, they'll have a better understanding of what the company is trying to do."

On our way back, David said, "What we need is a suggestion box. I think it would help us to communicate our ideas."

"I guess I should 'consider it done'." I smiled.

David laughed and said, "No, I don't know if I can get that done or even if I should."

I responded, "Well, if you're concerned about giving up your weekend to make a nice wooden suggestion box, the company will reimburse you. But there are simpler ways; you could take a shoe box, put a slot in the top and write 'SUGGESTIONS' on it."

David responded, "I could even use that box down by your foot (as he pointed to the brown box on the floor). Couldn't I?"

"You sure could," I said. "Your idea is better and even faster than mine."

The next day I told the people in the office about David's urgency in solving a problem, and it dawned on me. I could have gone one better than David, by saying, "I'll get the red pen and write 'SUGGESTIONS' on that brown box." But I was a day late. David had already taken care of it. 🔥

> *The value of an idea lies in the using of it.*
> *— Thomas Edison, inventor and entrepreneur*

THE MORAL OF THIS STORY

1. Why do most suggestion boxes fail? Maybe because only the boss or a few key leaders are allowed to open the box and answer the suggestions. Talk about your bureaucracy.

2. Everybody should open the suggestion box. Why are only leaders allowed to deal with the suggestions? If everyone participates, the urgency in addressing the suggestions will improve. People want a quick answer or they become unhappy because nobody listened or cared enough to answer their suggestion. The *success* of a suggestion box lies in the speed of the answer.

3. Consider it done! Why don't you take the action yourself? Why waste time stuffing your suggestion in the box? Maybe your suggestion should be answered by you. Use common sense and remember the core values. The value of an idea lies in the using of it.

15
Our Lobby

It was time for a facelift at Armstrong International, Inc., Michigan. Many of our departments (i.e. sales, engineering, production control, purchasing, accounting and marketing services) had received new carpet, office equipment and partitions for new office cubicles. Everything looked great and the company had a new image—or did it?

"Hi, Doris, how have you been?" I asked.

"Real good now that winter is over."

"Doris, do you…" (the switchboard lights up with six calls).

"Excuse me, David, while I take these calls."

I decided to wait on the couch where our guests sit. The couch looked uncomfortable. I sat down. It was. I glanced at the table covered with magazines and then looked at the ceiling. To my surprise, it was covered with water marks. I looked around the room. It was cluttered. The carpet was worn. The Armstrong logo was falling off the door. The couch was dirty and outdated. There was only one phone available and no privacy in the event someone wanted to visit with me. The lobby needed a facelift!

Doris hung up the phone.

"Doris, why don't you and your backup people, Billie Jo Kannenberg and Brenda Pobanz, submit a "wish list" of how you would remodel the lobby—keeping in mind Armstrong sells quality. Make the lobby first class."

Shortly thereafter, I received the wish list and approved it.

> *A perception is formed through many vehicles—*
> *sight, sound, smell, taste and touch.*

THE MORAL OF THIS STORY

1. The sight of the lobby... gave the perception of poor quality. The old looking couch, ceiling tiles with water spots and worn carpet said it all.

2. The touch of the lobby... gave the perception of a company tight on cash. The couch felt old, there were Styrofoam cups instead of glasses or cups, and the wet carpet under your feet said "Do they have money to pay me?"

3. The sound of the lobby... since the receptionist was out in the open it was noisy for Doris to answer the phone. I wonder what our customers thought on the other end of the phone as they heard people's voices in the background?

4. The smell of the lobby... nothing special, like the smell of flowers, coffee and cookies.

5. The taste of the lobby... nothing special, like cake, doughnuts and other goodies. The coffee should be top quality; made from fresh, ground coffee beans. Fudge at Christmas would be nice.

16
The Twilight Zone

You've just entered the twilight zone when you hear, "I hate my job. All I do is answer the phone, take orders, print reports and letters, and take complaints. It's so boring; I really hate my job! I can't keep up. I'm even working nights. Don't they realize I need help? Why won't they give me somebody who can help? Wait a minute... can it be? They're bringing in somebody new."

"Hi, my name is HP."

"It's nice to meet you. They call me Canon."

"Boy, I'm glad you're here. I've been so busy I can't keep up. Let me show you what to do."

The day ends when Canon says to HP, "What's that time clock above you, the one with the times for all the countries in the world?"

"Oh, they put that up as a reminder to everyone to respond to faxes as quickly as possible. In other words, if it's 8:00 a.m. in Michigan, it will be 2:00 p.m. in Belgium. We only have two, maybe three, hours to reply by fax to get an answer back the same day. Many people waited to answer the fax until afternoon (our time); therefore, it was already the next day for the customer.

"You know, HP, that's not only a smart thing to do for faxes, but also for returning phone calls."

"You're right! Canon, the only problem is that management needs to tell all the people what the time clock (by country) is for. Many people see it, but don't know its purpose."

Canon prints another piece of paper and says, "Isn't that always the case? Here we are… two time-saving fax machines. How many people think about picking up the faxes when we print them?"

"Very few; most people wait a half-hour or more," answers HP (Hewlett Packard). The whole purpose of our existence is to speed up communications between two parties? That time clock is like us—no good unless used properly." 🔥

Put yourself in your customer's shoes—better yet, time zone.

THE MORAL OF THIS STORY

1. If you can't afford expensive worldwide time clocks… what's wrong with buying cheap alarm clocks, setting each to a time zone and placing the name of the country on it? Start cheap.

2. "Day and night shift" should be removed from our company's vocabulary. When it's daytime in Japan, it is evening in the United States. If we want to better service our global customers, we should operate our business as if it were daytime always. I know this is expensive and few companies can afford it, but we should work our way toward this goal. Our next hire in engineering could be for the night shift.

3. "Domestic and international" should be removed from our company's vocabulary. There are no domestic or international markets anymore. The world is too small. Competition covers the world. When we use the word international, we tend not to give the same service or sincere consideration when making changes to our products, codes, method of payments, etc. Coca-Cola Company understands this and they have done away with the words *domestic* and *international*. So should we!

17
It Sounds Like Greek To Me

There they sat in the conference room at Armstrong International, Stuart, Florida, waiting for the consultant to arrive. My father had hired him to come and talk about a complex issue. In the room were top executives and department managers who had all gone to college. Many had several years of experience and understood business very well. The consultant arrived, spread out his sheets of paper on the table, and began to discuss the problem at hand. Throughout his talk, he used very complex words. A few were six syllables. It sounded like this man really knew what he was talking about. He talked for several hours. After he left, my father asked the group if anybody understood what had been said. Not to his surprise, the answer was,
"No."

For you see, my father also did not understand everything that had been said, and he was already well acquainted with the subject. 🔥

Some speak well, but never communicate.

THE MORAL OF THIS STORY

1. A large vocabulary is not a sign of intelligence. Just because you have large words in your vocabulary doesn't mean you are smart. We talk for one purpose — to communicate. Most people do not use large, complex words. Therefore, you shouldn't either. If you really know what you are talking about, you can use simple words. Let **what** you have to say impress people, not **how** you say it.

2. Know who you are talking to when choosing your words. Remember when computers first came out and specialists used fancy words we had never heard of before? Nano seconds, Bits, Disc, DOS, Server, Windows, etc. Remember how difficult it was to understand those specialists in the computer industry when they talked? Be careful you don't make the same mistake with your profession's nomenclature. Oooooops! Nomenclature *is* a big word. Buzz words or lingo says it better.

3. Old habits are hard to break. The words you use when speaking become habit. If you learn large unpopular words to communicate, you probably use them more than you realize during everyday conversation. This is just another good reason never to build your vocabulary with large words. If you have a small vocabulary, where most of your words are familiar, you never have to worry about which words to use.

4. Always take the time... to make sure you've been clearly understood. No matter what size words you use, be sure you've communicated what you intended. Good communication normally takes time — lots of time.

18
HELLO!

"**H**ello — Tom Henry speaking."

That's what you will hear when you call Tom Henry, Sales Manager at Armstrong Petro/Chem, Michigan. If you've ever heard Tom Henry's **hello,** you will know what I mean when I say it's full of energy, passion, and excitement. Tom sounds like he's having fun at work. Tom sounds like he's happy to speak to you. I for one am going to try to answer the phone more like Tom because I too enjoy my work and want the people who call me to have their spirits lifted.

Keep your eyes on things you cannot see.
— Confucius, philosopher

THE MORAL OF THIS STORY

1. What's better than answering the phone within three rings? Saying **hello** with *excitement* in your voice within three rings.

2. How should you hang up the phone when finished? Be careful not to slam the phone down when you're done. Many times people still have their phone to their ear and they hear that awful noise — slam! The impression you give is that you can't wait to hang up. Pause for one or two seconds before hanging up the phone. It will become a good habit.

3. Catch the spirit. Once you've caught the spirit from Tom's **hello,** help spread it by answering the phone with your own cheerful **hello.**

4. It's not what you say, but how you say it. I'm not talking about large vocabulary words. I'm talking about passion in your voice. The passion in your voice will tell the listener more than what you say. "Hey, this guy really enjoys his job!"

5. You create your own personal image by the way you answer your phone. Answering the phone as Tom does with excitement, energy, and fun in his voice, creates the image of a "can do" leader — a person whom you would like on your side.

Stories about core values

CHAPTER V

19
A Handshake

![black bar]

Armstrong International, Inc. and Yoshitake, Inc., Nagoya, Japan, reached an agreement; an agreement between Gus Armstrong and Susumu Yamada. Both presidents wanted their companies to grow in each other's country, thus each needed the other's distribution network.

Discussions took place and an agreement was made that Yoshitake-Armstrong would sell Armstrong's products, except humidifiers, in Japan. In return, Armstrong-Yoshitake would sell Yoshitake's pressure reducing valves (PRVs), strainers and other products around most of the world—primarily in the United States and Europe.

Three joint ventures were established: one each in Japan, the United States and Europe. Profits were split equally in all three joint ventures, in order to eliminate unfair advantage with fluctuation of yen versus the dollar or European currency and to simplify the division of the world market. To protect the joint ventures from the manufacturing plants making unfair profits, it was agreed all products sold to the joint ventures from Yoshitake or Armstrong would be sold at 15 percent above cost. It was also agreed that one day the joint ventures would be able to manufacture the products in their own country. For example, Armstrong-Yoshitake may want to manufacture PRVs in the United States or Europe.

When all was said and done and agreed upon, Susumu Yamada and Gus Armstrong stood up, extended their hands and finished the deal with a handshake. There was no written contract for quite some time. When the contract was written, it was under the same guidelines and rules that had been discussed. Since that first handshake of trust these two men have become good friends.

I feel honored to have been allowed to witness an agreement of this importance, made through the *simple* act of a handshake instead of a written contract. 🔥

> **There's no need to read the small print with a handshake.**

THE MORAL OF THIS STORY

1. "Do you have it in writing?"... should not be words from your mouth. If you gave your word, you must honor it. For example, you must pay your bills on time. You gave your word, and, just as important, the company's word. You keep your company's reputation and credibility by fulfilling what you promise, such as paying the bills. You will find that paying your bills on time gives you privileges (since many companies do not); vendors typically will provide you with better service and go that extra mile for you.

2. Be careful about vows you take. There are some vows you can break. For example, those that were immoral or illegal to begin with.

3. We must be "people of integrity." If the company's employees have integrity the company has integrity. If our company has integrity we can attract better employees, vendors and customers.

20
Somebody Read My Story

Steve Shutes, from production control, Armstrong International, Inc., Michigan, became concerned when he read my story on cartoons. To some readers, the original version of the story sounded like Armstrong-Yoshitake copied cartoons from other artists (without their permission) and proceeded to send these cartoons out in a calendar promoting Armstrong products. The truth of the story is that no such thing occurred.

Why was this a concern to Steve Shutes? Core values. Steve was concerned that we had violated copyright laws and thus broken a core value of legality. Steve was led to believe this through reading the story. He was so concerned, he took the time to draft a letter dealing with the legal ramifications of copyright violation and sent it to me because I was the author of the story.

I was so impressed with Steve's understanding of copyrights and the fact that he understood our core values, that I called him. "Steve, this is David Armstrong. I received your letter. I'm deeply impressed that you took time to read one of my stories and that you understand the true meaning of our core values. Your understanding of copyright laws is impressive. Steve, we never copied the cartoons from other artists and used them in the calendar. We discussed this with our legal counsel and saw the same problem you identified. I didn't change my story because the point I was trying to make was "Creativity," not core values. I'm sorry I misled you and the other readers. We will change the story so that we do not mislead readers in the future."

Steve replied, "David, thanks for calling. I didn't think we wanted to practice copyright violation after all the stories I had read on protecting our core values. Thank you for telling me what really happened and I'm glad you were not upset that I wrote you the letter."

I finished by saying, "Upset?— I'm proud of you, Steve! Whenever you see me or someone else doing something wrong, let us know." 🔥

> "Silence gives Consent."
> — Oliver Goldsmith, poet and playwright

THE MORAL OF THIS STORY

1. Why did only Steve take action to rectify this core value violation? I hope it's because nobody read my stories and not because they either don't know our core values or are afraid to say something when one is violated.

2. Nobody, but nobody, breaks a core value. Steve understands our core values: honesty, loyalty, fairness, safety, legality, and morality.

3. We must enforce them! Identifying a core value violation is one thing. Taking action is another. Steve took action to fix the problem—which is essential if our core values are to hold any meaning.

4. When someone takes their precious time to inform you or ask a question… you had better take your precious time to answer or explain what really happened. If you don't, the employee will be confused or feel you don't care. Why bother telling you *anything?* "Yes, I know you're too busy."

5. Steve was more concerned about the company breaking a core value than offending me. I like that—I like that a lot!

21
Bribes

Let me share a story my father told me in a faraway place. The story starts with a phone conversation my father had with a salesman.

The salesman said, "Thank you for taking the time to talk with me today."

"It's my pleasure," said Gus.

"By the way, are you happy with the free gifts we sent?"

"What free gifts are you talking about?"

The salesman continued, "Oh, you know, the wine, cigars, clothes, etc., we've been sending to your sales manager."

With confusion in his voice, Gus said, "I'm not aware of any free gifts."

The salesman explained, "Well, these gifts are sent often. It's common knowledge that your overseas sales manager expects to receive gifts in return for good service. Just ask any of the representatives."

Gus thanked the salesman for his time and said, "I will look into this matter. This is against company policy and we will stop it immediately! I was not aware this was going on."

Gus Armstrong confirmed the facts by calling several overseas reps, all of whom gave the same story... free gifts have been sent to the same sales manager for quite some time.

The sales manager was summoned to the president's office. Gus immediately questioned the sales manager—"I've just been informed you are receiving free wine, cigars and other gifts in return for service from our company. Are these stories true?"

"Yes, the stories are true and I'll be happy to stop accepting free gifts immediately."

Gus responded quickly, "No, you don't understand! You knew this was against company policy—I'm afraid today will be your last day."

> *Knowing is not the same as believing.*

THE MORAL OF THIS STORY

1. It's against company policy to accept bribes. You know when you're being bribed. If you don't know and you're *uncomfortable* with it, you better find out if it's a bribe or you could be fired. Here are a few tests to help you decide.

2. Would you want your gift described in a company newsletter? Would you feel comfortable telling everyone how you got your free gift and what it was?

3. Does it benefit *only* you or the company as well? If you accept a free lunch to *discuss* business, it benefits you *and* the company. That's acceptable.

4. Do you want to keep it a secret? If so, it's probably a bribe. Sooner or later, someone will mention that you're taking a bribe, so don't play the game. The cost is too high! It may cost you your job.

5. Does it pass the smell test? Some things can't be proven, but you know if it smells. Take milk, for example. It may look good, but if it smells you know better than to drink it. Trust your nose.

6. Is the gift a sample or a bribe? How do you know? Ask yourself if the *free* television was *manufactured* by the giver. If so, it's a sample; if not, it's a bribe. If it is a sample, make sure it's for the company and not just for your benefit.

7. In some countries bribes are acceptable. The wages in some countries are so low that bribes help supplement income. The country's government probably knows about these bribes and allows them. Allow the "supplier" in that country who lives there to offer the bribes. Armstrong should *not* offer bribes.

22
A Manicure

Many decades ago, V-belts were used to run machinery. Safety was a concern, even back then, but as with all machine shops, there were hidden dangers. Mr. Mohney was about to have his life changed forever and didn't know it.

Harold Mohney was working on his machine in the tool room at Armstrong International, Inc., Michigan. He was changing the V-belt to change the speed of his machine. Back then V-belts were used to change the speed of a machine since we didn't have gear boxes. Down the long aisle came a fellow worker named Bob. Bob was saying good morning to everyone when suddenly he heard,

"Owwww."

He quickly looked to where he heard the sound. There was Harold holding his hand up in the air with blood dripping down his arm. He was shaking his hand in the air like you do when you are in serious pain, hoping the pain will go away. Bob quickly ran over to Harold.

"Are you OK, Harold?"

"No—I think I cut my finger off."

Sure enough, he had cut off the tip of his finger.

Bob asked,

"How did you do that?"

Harold said,

"I was working on the V-belt and I just put my finger in, like this."

Suddenly, **zipppp,** they heard that awful noise. Harold had cut off *another* fingertip. ♨

> *Never make the same mistake twice.*

THE MORAL OF THIS STORY

1. It's your safety, use your best judgment. Don't wait for someone to tell you something is unsafe. Don't wait for someone to put in a safety feature to protect you and others. Use your best judgment. All the warnings and safety devices in the world are no replacement for common sense. It's your life, they're your fingers. You are as responsible as management for assuring that everyone is safe while working.

2. Fool me once, shame on you; fool me twice, shame on me. I love a good joke. Believe me, I have played enough jokes in my days to know when to appreciate a good one. One thing I am always careful of is that my jokes are safe jokes. When playing a practical joke on one of your fellow employees, be careful that it does not endanger them. How do you know? You know, just like the Native American boy knew he was picking up a rattlesnake in the story *Lead Us Not Into Temptation*, retold in my first book, *Managing By Storying Around.*

3. Danger...Warning...Keep Out. These signs are there for a reason. They are put there to alert you. Make no mistake — they do not assure safety. That is your responsibility. Signs only remind you of the potential danger. Unfortunately, common sights such as these signs become unnoticed. That is why I am bringing it to your attention again in the moral of this story.

4. Bring attention to the common sights. If you change the color, shape or location of your warning signs, or simply put new ones up, you will bring attention to them, and improve safety. If you have a safety problem at your company, try this. It just might work.

23
Four Eyes

Smack, smack, smack went his leather shoes against the cement floor as he ran through the plant. Grant Kain, plant foreman, was busy that day. He was in a hurry to get to his office. The sound of his feet hitting the cement came to a stop as he entered his office. Finding his chair, Grant fell into it, exhausted. While trying to catch his breath, he heard at his door—knock, knock. Looking up, he saw Ron Britton, machinist, and motioned Ron to come in.

"Grant, you must be really busy today."

Grant answered breathing hard,

"Yes—it's been a busy day. What can I do for you?"

"Well, Grant, you know you put me on the safety committee, and we're supposed to make sure everybody wears their safety glasses, and we're supposed to give warnings to those who don't. I'm giving you that warning. You didn't have any safety glasses on."

Grant's jaw fell and his mouth hung open while a blank expression came over his face.

"You're right, Ron. I didn't wear my glasses."

"Grant, you know management has been encouraging people to wear their safety glasses. It doesn't look good if management doesn't wear them and expects their people to."

"You're right, Ron. I simply forgot. Thank you for bringing it to my attention."

Grant smiled at Ron as he was leaving, with Ron smiling back.

Shortly thereafter, Grant was on his rounds in the shop, when off in the corner of the building, he saw Ron. Ron was away from all the machines and was reading something. Grant approached him.

"Ron, I noticed you're not wearing your safety glasses."

Ron smiled, "You're right, Grant, I should have them on, shouldn't I."

Grant gave a little laugh, turned around, and went on with his business. 🔥

> **Catch the smoking gun while it is still smoking.**

THE MORAL OF THIS STORY

1. Practice what you preach. It had been one year since a safety committee had been formed to enforce the wearing of safety glasses. Management was pushing for safety. Ron knew Grant had to live the message. Grant returned the favor to Ron when he also warned him. Remember, Ron was on the safety committee. We recently won an award for seven years with no major accidents. We were one of the few companies in the state of Michigan to receive such an award.

2. Don't kill the messenger. In most companies, Ron approaching his boss's boss in such a manner would be foolish for his career, since nobody likes to hear bad news—especially about oneself. I hope this story encourages our people to not be afraid to approach their co-workers with bad news. Remember, don't make it personal. Do it in a polite way. Guess who the storyteller was? I heard Grant Kain tell this story to some visitors one day.

3. A spare set of safety glasses. Make sure each of the doors to the factory is equipped with safety glasses, tissues, and cleaning solution. Make sure the safety glasses are in good shape so people will wear them. If glasses are dirty or scratched so you cannot see through them, they won't be worn. Safety glasses should have an inspection date just like fire extinguishers. Check their quality as well as quantity.

Stories

to

boost

creativity

24
Dragons, Leprechauns, Tooth Fairies and... ?

It was magical and mysterious. No one knew where it came from or how it got there. It just appeared one day at Armstrong International, Inc., Florida.

As the light sparkled off its gold horn, it caught your eye; you knew it had a purpose. You couldn't help yourself, you were drawn nearer and nearer—finally standing face to face with it. Its horn brought back memories, memories of your childhood days. You remembered reading about such an animal and thinking how marvelous it would be to see it running through the fields. As a child, you always hoped you would find one but never did. Here, today, as an adult, you stand before it, with a smile on your face thinking, "How foolish I was as a child to have believed in such a thing!"

Where oh where did this unicorn statue come from? This magical, mysterious unicorn that only children believe in. How did it find its way to Armstrong? 🔥

Trust your dreams, not your fears.

THE MORAL OF THIS STORY

1. The secrets of making dreams come true. Walt Disney revealed his secret in four "C's": curiosity, confidence, courage and constancy (freedom from change). The greatest of these is *confidence*. When you believe anything, believe in it all over, implicitly and unquestioningly.

2. Why did Walt Disney pick *confidence* as the greatest? As adults we do not have the confidence we had as children when it comes to believing in our dreams. To make your dreams come true, you must "believe," which gives you confidence.

3. "A great man is he who has not lost the heart of a child." Mencius, Chinese philosopher, 372-289 B.C., said this. Walt Disney gave good advice on *how* you make dreams come true. But how do you get people to dream? My solution is to place familiar statues, such as unicorns, where they will remind people to think as a child. Refer to my story "Signs," where I try to accomplish the same thing by using words. It is not easy to create an atmosphere that keeps people young in heart and mind.

4. The unicorn has a message. To make sure all understand that message of creativity, a plaque is attached with the words, "Dare to dream as a child." Long after we are gone, unicorns will still be found in the dreams of children. I hope the future will encourage more dreams of unicorns for adults.

5. A unicorn could be found anywhere...in the office, cafeteria, shop, or even at the main entrance. Find a place where the traffic of people is the heaviest. The more people who see it, the more will follow. You should also select locations where people most affected by the statue will see it. For example, if the statue is for innovation, place the statue near the R&D department.

25
Signs

Last week I took my family to Disney World. Long before we entered the grounds, a bright purple sign gave us directions. **"Purple,"** I thought to myself. "Who uses purple signs? It's gotta be a mistake." We drove a little further and again, up ahead, I could see another bright purple sign. "Purple, why is Disney using purple signs?" Then it occurred to me, "Disney is a **very special place!** Even the signs are special." When I saw the purple signs, I knew I was in the "World of Disney" where anything is possible. That's when it hit me: The *importance* of signs—not only for direction, but for creating an atmosphere.

Our family trip was over and I had just finished parking the rental car at the airport. I met up with my family in the terminal. As we were walking to our gate, I decided to make a quick stop in the restroom. As I approached the restroom, I saw a sign. This sign was in English and Spanish, but it also had a picture of a man. That's when it hit me; the airport had something in common with Disney—their signs. Whether I spoke English, Spanish or another language, it didn't matter because a **picture** conveyed the message, not the words. Once again, the importance of signs was made clear to me.

Then I asked myself, "If we want to become more international as a company, why do we have signs only in English? What about our foreign visitors? We need to change our signs so they are helpful to everyone! Upon my return, we redesigned our signs. 🔥

It's kind of fun to do the impossible.
— Walt Disney, Disney Corporation

THE MORAL OF THIS STORY

1. Signs create atmosphere. When you arrive at Armstrong International, Inc., Michigan and Florida, and see our different signs, you know you've entered a new and wonderful world of business and get caught up in Armstrong's atmosphere!

2. What makes a sign different? To begin with, the sign can be bright in color. Second, the way you hang the sign is important, such as by using a rope or chain. Third, the writing on the sign is important. What does it say? How does it say it?

3. Pictures speak a thousand words. "International" means we sell around the world; yet, our signs are in English and *only* English. Pictures are a universal language. We must add international symbols to our signs so everyone, regardless of their nationality, understands them.

4. Are your signs illegal or outdated? Have your general counsel review them to be certain. Do they use outdated words like "Powder Room?"

5. Use the new department names in your reports and when speaking. When you refer to the Engineering Department, don't say "Engineering," say "Imagineering." All reports and accounting records should indicate "Imagineering Department." The signs and what they stand for must become a part of our vocabulary to obtain the atmosphere we desire.

6. New signs must be explained. For a short period, talk up the sign, explain why the name was changed. Tell everyone who will listen. Then post what the new name stands for on the bottom of each sign. After a few months remove the explanation.

7. Go slow! Telling a customer you are the Director of "Imagineering" may be too much at first. *Go slow!* Start with your own people first.

8. Here are some names (which we use at Armstrong) you may want to copy:

"Engineering Department" to *"Imagineering."* Like Walt Disney, we've renamed our "Engineering Department" the "Imagineering Department" because, after all, engineers are supposed to use imagination when developing new products.

"Drafting and CAD Department" to *"Dimensioneering."* New technology, such as Computer Aided Design (CAD), allows draftspersons and engineers to stretch their imaginations through its simplification of the way they review and change their drawings. This simplicity and speed of change gets the ideas on the drawings before the engineers and draftspersons forget their ideas, thereby improving innovation, urgency and quality.

"Personnel" to *"Family Affairs."* We deal with *family.*

"Men" and *"Women"* restrooms to *"Boys"* and *"Girls."* Do you remember what it was like to be 12 years old? Think as a child. Children are caring, open minded, eager to learn, have fun and have lots of energy! With these traits, coupled with their curious minds, anything is possible! Yes, I said *anything* is possible. Think as a child. We need to hire children.

"Demonstration (Demo) Room" to *"Seeing is Believing."* Glass piping and see-through duct work allow customers, as well as employees, to witness our products or competitors' products under actual operation. Literature and test reports require *blind* trust by the customer, whereas "seeing" the product with one's own eyes speaks for itself.

"The Lobby" to *"Home Sweet Home."* Many who visit Armstrong comment, "I feel right at home; your people are so kind." Let's not forget it! This sign should help us remember.

"Domestic Sales & International Sales" to *"Global Sales."* We sell to the world and every nation should be equal in status. By doing away with *domestic* and *international*, all nations are equal.

"The Lab" to *"Tests Я Us."* The better, faster and the more we test, the better our chances of success with new, as well as current products.

"Drinking Fountain" to *"Perrier On Tap."* Some signs are just for fun, to make you laugh.

"Heat Treat Department" to *"Shake and Bake."* Visitors notice this sign and ask "why?"

"Incinerator" to *"Up In Smoke."*

"The Accounting Department" to *"Global Currency ($ - DM -£ - BF - Y=)."* Just like global sales, we want the accounting department to remember they finance projects, orders, salaries, etc. around the world. Using currency symbols helps remind them.

26
Two Camels in Mom's Living Room

Mom and Dad were preparing to leave for the day—but not until they gave our babysitter her final instructions. Of course, Tammy, my sister, and I knew the rules of the house. After all, Mom had been repeating them for the past eight years.

One "in the house" rule was that we weren't allowed in the "blue" living room! It received its name "blue" because of the blue carpeting. There was a black marble fireplace in the middle of this room. Mom told us not to play in the curtains for they were *very expensive!* And, of course, her most prized possession was her white velvet couch that we were *never, ever* allowed to sit on! There were plenty of rooms to play in but, of course, we couldn't resist the blue living room since it was *off limits*.

Now, Mom and Dad had left and the babysitter was busy caring for my younger brother, Patrick. This was our chance!

Tammy had a great idea. "Why don't we pretend we are camels in the desert? Let's pretend the blue carpet is hot sand."

So we got down on our hands and knees and pretended to be camels.

"This isn't fun," I thought to myself.

Then Tammy had a brilliant idea. "We need a sand storm!"

"That's a good idea," I said. Tammy asked, "But how can we do it?"

Being the older and "wiser" brother, I said, "I know," and I ran into the kitchen to grab the fan. I set the fan up in the living room and turned it on. "That's our sand storm. We can pretend the air hitting our faces is sand."

We played for a few more minutes and I said, "It's just not *real* enough. Wait a minute!" Then I ran into Patrick's room. Now Patrick wasn't very old, still in diapers, so I knew I could find what I needed in his bedroom. I came back to the living room and said, "Tammy, are you ready?"

"Yep, I'm ready." I turned the fan to HIGH and showed her the baby powder. Then I poured it into the fan. What a sand storm we had… white sand flying everywhere! And, of course, all over mom's beautiful blue rug, white velvet couch and black marble fireplace. We got down and played as the white sand flew through the air. But the powder began to burn our eyes, so we decided that wasn't a good idea. We turned the fan off.

Just then you could hear the babysitter running around the corner, **"What are you doing? What are you doing?"**

It was too late… the whole house was covered with white sand. 🔥

> *Creativity begins at home;*
> *encourage your children and learn from them.*

THE MORAL OF THIS STORY

1. Creativity does not need to be learned; you are born with it. As children, we are all good daydreamers and full of imagination. Why is it when we become adults—wise adults—imagination and creativity is foolish or, as some might say, "childish?" They're wrong!

2. "You're too old to behave like that!" Remember when you first heard that from your parents? *That's* how we stop being creative. Parents as well as the school systems need to encourage creativity. Heck, even colleges should require a "Creativity 101" class. Be careful what you say; the ability of our future leaders to dream depends on it!

3. Creativity has nothing to do with your age. Children are better at fantasizing, dreaming and creating, only because they practice it every day. Practice makes perfect. Get started!

27
The Dugout

1992 was the year Armstrong International, Inc., Michigan started changing their signs. *Conference Room A* and *Conference Room B* still hung above the doors in our basement. I sent a fax to Armstrong's executive staff offering two new names — The Sand Box and The Tree House. The next day I received a fax with their comments. It read,

"The staff went crazy about The Sand Box (sounds like a cat's litter box), The Tree House (tree houses aren't in basements).

"Ahhhh! I thought to myself, they just don't get it. It doesn't matter if a tree house is in the basement of the building. You're supposed to use your imagination. These words were disappointing to me. I had been trying for so long to build the imagination of our people. I wanted to throw the fax away, but I read further.

"The staff would like to propose the following names: 1) The Dugout; 2) The Bunker; 3) The Clubhouse; 4) Future World; 5) Rathskeller; and 6) The Confessional."

"Wow!" I thought to myself, "this is great. They're getting caught up in the spirit of using signs to promote an environment where fun and creativity can be the norm and not the exception."

I phoned Rex Cheskaty, general manager.

"Let's start with The Dugout. What do you think my next request is going to be?"

"You're going to want to decorate the rooms to match the names," Rex answered.

"You got it. Let's remember always to keep things simple and small, so if it fails we can go back to the way it was, quickly, with little expense."

Rex interrupts; "We've already started decorating the room— we knew you would like that. We have some real good ideas. Imagine, David, if you walked through the door and you immediately found yourself in a dugout. When you step out you walk onto green AstroTurf with white lines drawn on it, representing a baseball diamond. On the one wall you will find stadium seats that seat 10 people, which we could use for training sessions. On the other wall might be a painted mural of the fans. Heck, they could be doing the wave. On the other wall you would have a bunch of lockers. And then of course you have the table shaped like a baseball bat where we sit for the meeting."

"Don't forget the peanuts and popcorn," I said. "We could leave baseball bats, gloves, and balls lying around. And just imagine, if we wanted to recognize our partners, our customers, we could present them not with a plaque which everybody gives, but a baseball autographed by the staff. Wouldn't that stand out when they took it back to their companies? Finally, we might want to put a big TV screen above the field like they do at the ball parks and use our CAD Solids Program to display new products to customers, or for slides and videotapes for training sessions. All these tools can be used to run our business and yet be fun and fit the atmosphere that we are trying to create." 🔥

If you want to make enemies, try to change something.
— Woodrow Wilson, 28th President, United States

THE MORAL OF THIS STORY

1. If your change isn't big enough, revolutionary enough, the bureaucracy can beat you. Jack Welch, CEO of General Electric, believes this and so do I. Dugouts, signs, storytelling, statues, are just the beginning.

2. Rookies and interviewees sitting in The Dugout. Imagine the impact on the person you are hiring when they sit in this creative atmosphere. Their thoughts will be, "Boy, this place must be fun. Management and the people really get along. I hope I get this job." You have an advantage that other companies do not have in hiring good talent. If they think this is childish and they want nothing to do with it, better they know it now than after they are hired. If you have the unpleasant task of firing someone, imagine another conference room that is peaceful and quiet. A water fountain, birds chirping, lots of colorful vegetation. You now have a choice of a peaceful environment, or the environment of the dugout with lots of action, creativity and enthusiasm.

3. Ability may get you to the top, but it takes character to keep you there. Mr. John Wooden, coach of the UCLA basketball team, was referring to each of his players when he said this. Many of Armstrong's companies are number one in their industry. That's because we have quality products, provide great service and are fast innovators. But it takes more than that to stay at the top. It takes character. The character I'm referring to can be summed up in the following words: having fun, having pride, loving change, and having a passion for urgency.

Stories
of
the
future

CHAPTER VII

28
Free Porterhouse Steaks

You're waiting in line at Johnson Corporation's JOCO Center for your dinner. As you pick up your plate and silverware, you see the salad. You then put a potato with plenty of butter on your plate. You add a piece of bread. Oh, what the heck, two pieces, and your dessert. You then walk over to the open pit and pick the steak of your choice. You think to yourself (as you look at your plate of food), "What could be better than this? Seconds, of course! Even better, it's free." After you've eaten more than you should, you slowly head toward the game room where a good game of poker, pool, and other entertainment await. The evening ends.

The next day you find yourself talking to others who went to the JOCO Center the night before.

"Hey, Bob, when is it time for Armstrong to have the Johnson people over at Armstrong International, Inc., Michigan for free steaks?"

"Sometime toward the end of the summer, I think."

"Are we going to have it at our recreation hall, like last year?"

Bob smiles, "The last I heard we were. It's a perfect location. We can cook the steaks outside, eat inside the gymnasium and proceed to the game room for some cards or bumper pool. Who knows, we might even get a game of basketball started."

"Bob, what did we do before Armstrong built the recreation building in 1986?"

"We had the steak frys outside, but it was never as nice as going to Johnson's JOCO Center. Their building was full of fun!" 🔥

> *Good help is hard to find—even harder to keep.*

THE MORAL OF THIS STORY

1. Keeping your people is difficult. Many companies focus on tangible incentives such as good pay, performance bonuses, health benefits, dental plans and supplemental retirement programs. Armstrong is no different. Armstrong offers many of these programs at its divisions. People are Armstrong's most valuable asset.

2. Don't forget the intangible incentives. A recreation building can be an incentive, especially during the winter months. It may keep your people from moving to a warmer climate or to a company that has this type of facility. How many companies do you know that offer recreation and fun as an incentive to keep their people? How many more intangibles can we offer?

3. Make it a family affair. Armstrong's recreation building can also be used by the employees' families. What was originally a benefit for our employees is now a benefit for their families. Here's another good reason to stay at Armstrong.

29
Listen to the Mockingbird

This story is dedicated to Ken Clay, Pat Steffey, Carolyn Masnari, Jerry Henry and Grant Kain, all members of the Oasis Team.

T here I was—in the middle of the park. I could still see the people in the streets and stores. The sky was a soft blue with a few clouds. I looked at the trees. They appeared to be reaching for the clouds. Amongst the green were patches of color from all the flowers. The park was peaceful and inviting.

I spotted a park bench with a lamppost just ahead. I could hear water falling from a fountain, but I didn't know where. I stopped at a drinking fountain which was obviously there for thirsty travelers. As I took a cool drink, I heard the sound of what appeared to be a mockingbird singing.

A few more steps brought me to the public restroom for the "Boys." I could smell food coming from a small café. The canopy over the windows blocked the blinding light for the customers' comfort. There was no grass in this park, nor was there dirt, just some stones and tile. This park can only be found inside the factory at Armstrong International, Inc., Michigan. 🔥

A visionary is never in his/her time.

THE MORAL OF THIS STORY

1. Is it safe in the park? Yes, even at night during the night shift. When I told Grant Kain, plant foreman, and Jerry Henry, general foreman, about my idea to build a park inside the factory, I expected Grant and Jerry to laugh me out of the building, maybe even commit me to the "funny farm." You can imagine my surprise when they jumped on the idea with excitement and a desire to make it even better! That's when they moved the location of the park, which I had on a quiet aisle, to a more heavily trafficked area and at the same time closed the aisle to fork truck traffic, thus improving safety. Before the park this aisle was always a concern because of safety problems. We had mirrors hanging from the ceiling on blind corners to show a fork truck coming and lights to signal a door being opened into the aisle. The fork truck drivers went slowly and used their horns when coming down the aisle. People were told to look both ways before entering the aisle, but there was always that fear of somebody getting hit by a fork truck. No longer—we now have a park.

2. A change of scenery... This park is located on the main aisle in the factory and it's approximately 30 feet long. It is the main path for office and shop people, visitors and customers, and is located in front of the bathroom and cafeteria. In other words, this path is heavily traveled. It is the perfect location for a park so everyone can enjoy and be affected by it. What is the effect, you ask? By installing this park, we hope to improve people's outlook. During the long winter months it is refreshing to walk in a park full of green vegetation and color. It is also pleasant in the summer when you prefer to be outside, not inside working. While walking through the shop you feel confined by the walls. All of a sudden, you enter this park and you have 30 feet of enjoyment which magically takes you away from your working environment. We hope this will help create a feeling of comfort, happiness, and peace of mind.

3. I'm proud to be an Armstronger! Our visitors at Armstrong International, Inc., Michigan have always been impressed at how clean our factory is and that we can leave money and food in the cafeteria unattended. We always hear, "We could never do this in our plant!" We take great pride in knowing we do something no one else can do. We will always be grateful to hear those comments, but it is time—it is time for something new; something we can brag about—a park! Who knows? In the future, all factories may have parks for employees to enjoy.

30
All We Have Is Our Name

Shortly after we had changed sales representatives in a territory, a new salesman was making a visit to one of our larger customers. The customer had placed a large order for customized coils produced by Armstrong-Hunt, Inc., Florida. Its purchasing department had designated Armstrong as the sole source for the products in question.

"Are you pleased with that last order we gave you?" asked the purchasing agent.

"Which order are you referring to?" replied the salesman.

"The one we gave you last month which is due to ship next week."

"I'm not aware of any orders placed with Armstrong-Hunt. Let me make a call." The salesman for Armstrong-Hunt confirmed that no order had been placed.

"Who did you give this order to?"

"The order was given to the local Armstrong-Hunt distributor."

The salesman explained that this person was no longer the authorized Armstrong-Hunt representative.

"I'm confused, let me look into this," said the purchasing agent.

Immediately, the customer called the local distributor where the order for Armstrong-Hunt had been placed. The distributor confirmed it had not forwarded the order for Armstrong-Hunt products to Armstrong-Hunt, but had given the order to another manufacturer. The local distributor claimed that it had notified the customer that it was changing vendors. However, after investigating the matter, the purchasing department determined that no one had known about, authorized, or approved the substitute product. If the new salesman had not made a call that day, the customer would never have realized they were not getting Armstrong-Hunt products.

Later on, the customer decided to accept one shipment of the substitute products due to the need for a prompt delivery. Upon receipt of the order, the customer's engineering department determined the product was not built to specifications and was inferior to the Armstrong-Hunt product. They returned it to the distributor.

When this was brought to Armstrong's attention, immediate action was taken. We filed suit against this distributor for interfering with Armstrong-Hunt's business relations.

One of our most valuable assets is our company's name.

THE MORAL OF THIS STORY

1. All we have is our name. We have spent 90 years building the Armstrong name as a symbol of quality and service. We cannot allow anyone to tarnish Armstrong's position in the market. Our future and much of our company's market value rests in our name.

2. All we have is our name. We cannot allow competition or anyone else to *reposition* our name. The fact that the distributor substituted an inferior product when the customer expected to receive an Armstrong-Hunt product not only interfered with our business relations, but posed a serious threat to our image as a quality producer for today and the future.

3. All we have is our name —our reputation and pride. Absolutely no one will tarnish our name. Those who try will answer for their actions. All the resources at Armstrong's disposal will be used to stop them. Our future depends on it.

Stories
to
honor
partnerships

31
Fly Like an Eagle

"Everlasting Valve had a vendor who went on strike," says Jim Bundy, purchasing agent of Everlasting Valve Corporation in New Jersey, as he begins his story. "During this strike, several of their people left the factory. The rep also went on his own. Several months later, he approached me, representing Eagle Alloy, and asked if I would give them a try. After Mark Fazakerley, vice president of Eagle Alloy, called me, I decided to give them a few patterns. They did a really good job on quality and delivery. They were very responsive to our needs, so I gave them a few more patterns—and a few more. Now, we give all of our work to Eagle Alloy. Eagle Alloy specializes in shell casting versus sand work. This means their tolerances are better and give us a smoother finish. That's good for our CNC machines."

A few months pass and the phone rings, "Jim Bundy speaking."

The purchasing manager at Armstrong International, Inc., Michigan responds, "Jim, this is Jerry Phelps. What's the scoop on these guys at Eagle Alloy? The representative in Michigan told me they sell to you?"

"Jerry, I'm real happy with them. Their service and quality are excellent! I really encourage you to give them an order."

"Well, we've had some problems and we need a good steel foundry. We'll give them an order and see how they do."

Several months pass and Jerry Phelps gives them another order, followed by another order, and within one year Jerry has given all of the steel business at Armstrong to Eagle Alloy. He has now made them a partner for Armstrong.

More time passes and another division of Armstrong International, Inc. enters the story.

"Jerry, this is Kathy Ardner at Warrick Controls. We just had a foundry close and we are in desperate need of steel castings. Do you have a good vendor we can use?"

"I've got just the foundry! It's Eagle Alloy. We started using them two years ago and now they're a partner. Let me send your patterns to Eagle Alloy with ours."

"Thanks, Jerry. We could really use a good vendor."

Over the past few years Eagle Alloy has gone from servicing one of Armstrong International's divisions to three. They have even earned the status of "partnership" at one of our divisions.

> *Let your partners make money—*
> *you want them to stay in business.*

THE MORAL OF THIS STORY

1. Share your successes. Eagle Alloy started with Everlasting Valve and that success was shared with Armstrong International, Inc., Michigan which in turn was shared with Warrick Controls. You are *not* competing with your sister divisions, so share your successes.

2. What attracts a good partner? Paying your bills on time for a start. You could also give your partner all of your business that exhibits total commitment. If your volume of business is small, remember you're talking about a partnership over many years. So if you only average $800,000 per year and you multiply that by 10 years, you're worth $8 million to that partner.

3. Partnerships must be built on trust. How do you build trust? Familiarity for a start. If the partner is a family-owned business, like your company, you have something in common. If the way they go to market (such as through reps) is the same as your company, you have something in common. Being familiar creates trust because you understand each other.

4. Partners cannot read your mind. Evaluation of partnerships is important. You should evaluate your partner at least once a year. They should also review you. When evaluating your partner, make sure to focus on those items most important to you. If your company's vision is *quality*, track scrap; if *urgency*, evaluate their responsiveness to your questions and deliveries.

5. Does your literature sell your partner? It's possible to display your partner's name on your product. If the casting has your partner's name on it, did you have it facing the camera or was it hidden?

32
Partnership Pin of Trust

It was a beautiful Hawaiian morning as my family went through the double doors to the conference room of the Westin Hotel on the island of Kauai. As the doors opened we saw a round table with 30 staff people representing each department of the hotel. We took the honorary seats and listened as each of the hotel's departments told us what they were going to do to service Armstrong International, Inc. during our Hawaiian convention. At the end of the meeting, the general manager approached my mother and father with two stick pins that had the logo of the Westin Hotel on them.

"Mr. and Mrs. Armstrong, we would like to present to you these stick pins, which will give you complete access to any department or help you fill any need you might have at the Westin Hotel. These stick pins give you complete freedom as if you were an employee of the Westin Hotel. By simply showing your stick pin, you will be able to have your needs fulfilled during your convention." I looked over at my mother and father and could see the impact this had on them.

Nine months later, I was on a tour inspecting our new lobby in Three Rivers, Michigan.

I asked, "Are the visitors using the phone and watching our videotapes on the new television?"

Our receptionist, Pam Alphenaar, answered, "Yes, they really appreciate having a telephone to use and they're using their credit cards just as we had hoped."

"How about the free cookies?"

"Oh yes, some of them even take a cookie to go."

"Wow, that coffee smells great!"

"Thanks, I brought in some gourmet coffee that my husband's company makes. It went over so well that we're buying it now instead of regular coffee."

"Where is the copy of our storybook, 'Managing by Storying Around?'"

"Right there... oops, someone took it again. I'll get another copy."

I said, "You know, I just had a great idea! Why don't we offer our partners a stick pin, which gives them complete access to any department within our company? This was done at the Westin Hotel and you wouldn't believe the goodwill it generated between my parents and the Westin. I think I'll have Helen Greene order the pins.

Remember, Pam, *only* our partners can receive them." 👥

> *Partnership stick pins are like Cinderella's Godmother's magical wand—anything becomes possible.*

THE MORAL OF THIS STORY

1. Adopt your vendor and customer partnerships into your family. The person wearing the partnership pin becomes part of our family. Becoming part of the family helps them feel that we care...and as a family we will do anything to help them.

2. We trust you. What better way of showing this than by giving this pin that provides access to our company without restrictions. Well...there may be a few restrictions, like how much I'm paid.

3. How do you know what restrictions apply? "A need to know" answers the question. If the stick pin partner needs to know or see something in order to service us, show them.

4. Don't let it be taken for granted. The more visible the pin is, the more often it is worn, the more it is noticed. The simple act of pinning reminds the partner they're special. The pin is very noticeable and is a constant reminder of our partnership, not only for our people, but also for the partner who wears the pin. We keep the pin in the receptionist's desk; it must be requested and returned when the partner leaves.

5. Keep them under lock and key. Only a select few should wear the pin, which makes it special. If it's special, the person wearing it feels honored and trusted. Guard those stick pins with your life.

6. Using a good idea is better than thinking of it yourself. The Westin Hotel had a great idea and we copied it. I hope you will copy the idea from this story for your division.

7. So...what does the pin look like? Look on the next page and you will see.

PARTNERSHIP

33
R.S.V.P.

Only a few months remained before the sales convention in Hawaii. Suddenly, we realized we had left someone very important off the list of invitations. Carpenter Technology had been a partner with Armstrong International, Inc., Michigan for over six years and supplied most of the stainless steel for our products.

Jerry Phelps, Armstrong's purchasing manager, called Gordon Wesley, special account manager for Carpenter Technology.

"Gordon, this is Jerry Phelps. Would you be interested in going to Hawaii in May as a guest of Armstrong?"

"Why me?"

"We have a sales convention and we feel it would be beneficial for both Carpenter Technology and Armstrong if you could see our new products. Many of these products use stainless steel which you sell. Maybe you will have some good ideas about our designs, welding or machining of your stainless steel."

"I'm ready to go. You're right, I could learn a lot about Armstrong and how to better serve you. This also gives me a chance to talk with your salesmen and leaders. It's a great idea."

"Gordon, if you want to bring your wife you can. You'll have to pay for her airfare, but Armstrong will cover all her other expenses. As for you, everything is paid by Armstrong. The convention will last one week."

"I'll be happy to pay for my wife's airfare and we will go when you're going, Jerry, so you can introduce us."

THE MORAL OF THIS STORY

1. Partnerships are a continuous journey. We do not stop with the simple act of signing a contract. You must nurture the relationship. By inviting Gordon to our convention, we did that.

2. Build upon your wins. The partnership with Carpenter Technology has been very successful for the past six years. We wish to build upon this experience. The word will travel that Carpenter Technology attended the Armstrong convention. This will motivate other vendors to become partners with Armstrong.

3. This was not a bribe. We called Carpenter Technology for their permission before inviting Gordon. We did not want Carpenter Technology to think we were trying to bribe Gordon in hopes of gaining better pricing. Remember those core values.

4. Another small start. This was the first time we had invited a partner to a sales convention. We wanted to start with one partnership to save money if it didn't work. It was a big success and we intend to invite more partners to the next convention.

Stories
to *honor*
quality and
service

CHAPTER IX

34
Self-Inspection

Three days had passed since Jim Bellew started working for Armstrong International, Inc., Michigan. It was his third evening when I first met Jim working the second shift.

"Hello, Jim. My name is David Armstrong. I want to welcome you to our family."

"It's nice to meet you," he answered. Jim quickly turned around as he put the next casting into the fixture to be machined.

"What do you know about quality?" I asked.

"In my previous job I was told quality is very important, that we should take pride in our work and only make a good product. I was also told I would be fired if I scrapped more than two pieces."

"Really?" I asked. "Was that for one day?"

"No, that was for one year."

"I'll bet you and the others hid your scrap so you wouldn't get fired."

"That's right," Jim laughed.

"Jim, that might be the way your past employer controls quality, but passing bad quality to Armstrong customers will *really* get you in trouble. We understand you will make mistakes and encourage you—no, DEMAND you to identify scrap and then find out why we have scrap. Don't hide it, thinking you're protecting your job. Sooner or later, someone will notice."

Jim asked, "That's really the way it is here, isn't it?" Jim then reached into a tray of good parts, retrieved a questionable casting he had machined earlier and put it into a tray marked "scrap."

"I'm proud of you, Jim. That's the way we do things at Armstrong!" 🔥

> *A company's quality is known by its past reputation, not by its newest quality program.*

THE MORAL OF THIS STORY

1. Learn from your mistakes. Armstrong learned a long time ago that a quality control department *does not assure* quality. We decided to make each and every person responsible for their own quality through self-inspection. Refer to my story, "The Bluetag Special" in *Managing by Storying Around*, Doubleday Currency, March 1992, for more details.

2. "SPC," "ISO-9000" and "TQM" are new versions of a quality assurance department. These programs do provide a means to *improve* quality, but they do not assure you will have quality. Once again, quality must come from our people. Remember the Japanese Quality Circles in the '70s? It's amazing we don't hear anyone talk about that today. It was a fad and, quite possibly, these new programs are also fads. Let's learn from them, but remember—people give us quality.

3. The blind leading the blind. Most new fads come from companies that have quality problems (or so I believe). If your company has good quality, don't lose it by blindly following a company that created the latest fad to fix their quality problems. Stay focused on what gives you quality, not on a program that is popular today.

4. Remind people what works. Jim was new at Armstrong. Obviously, I had beaten his foreman and fellow workers in discussions on quality. If people don't know what is expected of them, they can't follow your company's philosophies. In most cases, they will follow what they learned at another company. Do you want to follow another company's policy on quality or your own? Be sure to take the time to tell new and current employees how you maintain quality products and service.

35
Seals at Lake Okeechobee

Some of the best fishing in Florida is found at Lake Okeechobee. It should come as no surprise that Computrol in Idaho (manufacturer of Bottom Line fish finders) considers this a location to sell their products.

Great business opportunities normally involve a number of problems. The problem with selling fish finders near Lake Okeechobee was seals. We're not talking about seals that eat fish or balance a ball on their nose. We're talking about rubber seals which are used to protect fish finders from the corrosive outside environment.

Through the years, Computrol has established several distributors. The distributor that covers the territory near Lake Okeechobee purchased one TBL-110XT fish finder. Within a short period of time it failed. A second unit was provided at no charge. It failed. A third unit was delivered, again at no charge. It failed.

With each occurrence of failure, Hazen Kreis III, district sales manager, would replace the unit the same day. He would also ask questions on how the unit failed—trying to determine the cause of failure. When the third unit failed, he determined that the seal leaked and humidity was entering the crystal display. He upgraded the unit (at no extra cost) to the 4400 Species Select—a unit that has better seals and sells for more.

Hazen called Computrol to discuss the situation. Could it be possible that designing and manufacturing the unit in Meridian, Idaho, (where the humidity is low) and selling the unit in other parts of the country (where the humidity is high) could be the problem? The problem only involved the TBL-110s. Hazen gave the serial number of each unit to Computrol in case a bad batch was manufactured during that day of production. 🔥

> *Take care to service your customer*
> *before taking the next order...*
> — *Adam Armstrong*

THE MORAL OF THIS STORY

1. **"Turning lemons into lemonade."** Not only did Hazen *immediately* (same day) rectify the problem of leaking seals with the distributor, he also upgraded the unit (4400 Species Select) at no extra cost. The distributor had reason to be upset, but to receive prompt service from Hazen and Computrol must have made the situation tolerable and likely a positive experience. Let's face it, there are few companies today that *truly* service their customer in such a manner.

2. **Employees close to customers are the first to find out about problems.** Listen to them—better yet, empower them—even better, insist they take authority and service the customer. If you take care of your customers, they will be with you for a lifetime.

3. **To err is human...** to fix the cause of the problem *permanently* is divine (Hazen upgrading the unit to a 4400). Nobody likes to be serviced for the same thing more than once.

36
Something Smells Fishy

It was near Christmas time when she found herself in the fishing department. As she walked down the aisle, she came across Computrol's Bottom Line fish finders.

A salesman quickly noticed her interest in the fish finders and approached her, "Can I help you with anything?"

"Yes," as she pointed to a unit in the corner of the display case. "I was just looking at that fish finder. Can you explain it to me?"

The salesman replied, "The Bottom Line fish finder is very user friendly. It has a menu selection which appears on the screen and walks you through the different features of the unit. You will also notice the screen is very large, which makes it easy for the fisherman to see what's going on. The clarity and resolution are excellent! This is the newest unit on the market with many special features that other units do not have."

The salesman looked for a nod of agreement before he continued, "There is a one-year warranty on the product from date of purchase. If you have any problems during that time, Bottom Line offers a 48-hour return policy. You just send your unit to the factory, call the factory that same day and they will send you a replacement by second-day mail. That's real important, especially if your husband is in a fishing tournament or has a fishing weekend coming up and his unit doesn't work."

As he lifts the unit for her inspection, he adds, "Another special feature is, for a nominal fee Bottom Line will update the software package in your unit. This way you don't have to buy a new unit when it becomes outdated. At present, for example, an update on an older model would cost approximately $100. Would you like me to wrap this up?"

As she looks at the unit one more time, she replies, "Yes, would you please? I know my husband will enjoy this and I can't wait to give it to him for Christmas." 🔥

> *Niching is not only done by your product features, but also through repair parts, service features, your people, advertising, market distribution and so on.*

The Moral Of This Story

1. Your product features should create a niche. Special features should be added to your product to *differentiate* it from competing products. There is no such thing as a commodity product. Everything can be *differentiated*.

2. Your products' parts should create a niche. Product features are not the only way to create a niche. You can provide a niche of service. To offer a 48-hour turnaround on repairs is a special niche. Most people who fish want their fish finder repaired in a few days and don't want to wait and risk missing a future fish outing.

3. Your service should create a niche. Computrol's Bottom Line fish finder's software can be rewritten to new technology for a small fee. Technology is changing so fast today that often when you buy a new product within a short period of time (too short for most of us), you find out the item you just purchased is outdated. And, let's be honest, that bothers us because we just spent a great deal of money. Deep down inside, we know it can be fixed or upgraded; they just want us to buy a new unit. Service is a niche.

37
Window Shopping

Rex Cheskaty is a good friend of mine. Rex's mother lives in the western part of the United States.

Mrs. Cheskaty loves to sightsee with her husband. They own a sports van and they drive around various states in the West.

Since Rex is a good friend of mine, he is aware of our companies and their locations. Like all good sons, he calls his mother often—sometimes three times a week.

During one of their sightseeing trips, Mr. & Mrs. Cheskaty found themselves in Meridian, Idaho, on the doorstep of Computrol. There was one problem—it was Saturday morning and Computrol was closed. Mrs. Cheskaty thought to herself, "Well, let's not waste this trip," and began to window shop. As she pressed her nose against the window trying to see in, a custodian appeared.

As the custodian opened the door, he asked, "Can I help you?"

"My son told me about your company, so when we found ourselves in the area we decided to take a look."

Not wanting to lose the opportunity to promote the Bottom Line fish finders, he said, "Please wait." He disappeared behind the door.

A few minutes later he returned, "I'm sorry we're closed, but please take these brochures on our fish finders with you." 🔥

> *Everything being done today will be done better tomorrow.*
> — *Moral #4*

THE MORAL OF THIS STORY

1. A newly built plant begins to depreciate the day it opens. The well-served customer, on the other hand, is an appreciating asset. Every small act (opening the door) on her behalf increases the odds for repeat business, add-on business and priceless word-of-mouth referrals."— Words of wisdom spoken by Tom Peters.

2. Word-of-mouth advertising costs nothing. Our custodian opened a door on Saturday morning and gave brochures to Mrs. Cheskaty (which cost almost nothing) and created word-of-mouth advertising.

3. Going the extra mile. Our custodian could have hidden in the shadows of the office and never opened the door. After all, it was Saturday and who would expect anyone to be in the building? He could have said to himself, "I'm not paid enough to do this. It's not my job and it's Saturday." He opened the door and happily greeted Mrs. Cheskaty and exhibited additional initiative in giving her brochures.

4. "If you don't do it, I will."— Your competitor.

38
Rush Job

Believe it or not: Don English, assistant foreman, Armstrong International, Inc., Michigan, told me he didn't have time to talk to me that morning. It all began when I received a message that Don English wanted to speak to me. I had already tried twice that week to talk to him, but both times he was gone. On my third visit to his department I found him hard at work welding a manifold. I waited until he was finished, then interrupted him.

"Don, I have a message you want to speak to me?"

"It wasn't that important. You didn't have to get back to me this quick."

"That's OK," I said. "When I'm in town I like to take care of my messages so people don't think I forgot."

"David, I hate to say this but I can't talk right now. I've got this rush job and we've got to get it out today. I've already spent eight hours on it and I'm going to need two hours of overtime just to finish it. Could you come back later and talk to me?"

I smiled. "That's no problem, Don. I'll come back tomorrow and talk with you when you have more time." I continued my journey through the shop. 🔥

> *He who wishes to secure the good of others*
> *has already secured his own.*
> — *Confucius, philosopher*

THE MORAL OF THIS STORY

1. Who is more important—the owner of the company or the customer? The owner wouldn't have a company if it weren't for the customer, so the customer is always number one. If the customer comes before the owner, then the customer comes before *everybody* in the company.

2. What was Don English thinking of when he told me to come back later? The next day I met with Don and his first words were, "I'm sorry I didn't talk with you yesterday. After you left I started thinking maybe that wasn't a good idea or the right thing to do." I said, "Don, don't apologize. I took pride in the fact that you sent me away to service our customer. That's what got you to the position of assistant foreman and that very same attitude will make you foreman one day."

3. If you want more people like Don in your company... you have to talk it up. I told five people that very day what Don had done. I made sure that the message was clear. I told them how proud I was of Don. I am writing this story to share with you what it takes to be promoted.

39
The Mighty Fisherman

Two fish are overheard talking:

"Did you hear the good news?"

"No."

"Mitch Riley can't go fishing today."

"All right! You know, last week he caught a few of my friends and had them for dinner. It's not like Mitch to miss a beautiful Saturday morning. Did you hear why?"

"It's got something to do with work."

It was 6:00 a.m. Saturday morning when Mitch met the truck driver.

"You didn't have to buy me breakfast," Mitch said.

"It's our pleasure, Mitch. Not too many people would give up their Saturday, and especially a fishing trip on the Gulf, to satisfy a customer. It's not your fault that the truck *we* had scheduled broke down causing a delay of two days."

"Robert I. Warden is Armstrong-Hunt's sales representative, and when they told us they had an order going to Denver Rio Grande Railroad, and that it was imperative the order was received on time, I knew the fish could wait. Besides, I caught a *whole bunch* last time I went."

By 9:00 a.m. that morning the truck was loaded and pulling out of the loading dock at Armstrong-Hunt, Milton, Florida. Several days later Mitch received a special shipment from Beau

Warden, president of R. I. Warden. Six jars of Robert I. Warden's famous "Blatant Heat" salsa was sent with the message **"Enjoy! **_With our compliments for servicing our customer, Beau Warden."_ 🔥

> *Ask not what your company can do for you,*
> *ask what you can do for your company.*

THE MORAL OF THIS STORY

1. Does this quote sound familiar to you? If you substitute the word *country* for *company* you will recognize it as the quote President Kennedy used in his inaugural address. Mitch's story reminded me of this quote. Your company does many things for you. Don't be afraid to ask what you can do for your company. Mitch coming in on a Saturday and giving up his fishing trip is a good example.

2. Does this story sound familiar to you? I'm sure it does. Just replace Mitch's name with a new name and change the events in the story and you would find one more story about servicing our customers. There are hundreds of stories on providing service to our customers beyond the call of duty. We almost take these stories for granted. The danger in this is that we soon forget to praise the people who make this possible. These stories must be retold even if the moral of the story is the same: service beyond the call of duty.

40
The Revolving Door

"They came by the hundreds. Sometimes in groups of five, but often one by one. What started as 10 soon was 50, then 100, 200, 300; the final count—330. They left as quickly as they came, seldom having time to exchange words, or even their names."

"Who were these people?" I ask.

"They were the new employees that Everlasting Valve Corporation, New Jersey, hired between the years 1974 and 1980."

(This would not have been a concern if Everlasting Valve employed 10,000 employees, but it didn't. It had only 15.) Doug Allcock, Shop Steward, looks out into the shop as he continues telling me his story.

"Sometimes we went through as many as five people in one week."

"Why do you think our turnover is so small today?" I ask.

"The pay is much better, and the benefits have improved. I think that's real important when hiring good people, which we have today. Almost no one has left in the last four years. Why don't you ask the others and see what they think?"

I saw John Caulfield.

"Hi, John. Why do you think the people are staying today?"

"Well, I agree with Doug. I also think the way this place is laid out helps. It's much more organized today. When a job is frustrating, it's tough to stay. Several of us stay because we remember the way it used to be in the old building at Cranford, New Jersey, back in 1974 through 1980. That was before Armstrong International, Inc. bought us. A better pension, a bonus plan, better pay and cleanliness. They all matter."

Roger Jensen, plant foreman, was leaving his office.

"Roger, I've got a question for you…"

"David, I've been here 25 years, and if anybody knows, it's me, and, of course, the other guys, John Caulfield, Bill Romeo, Doug Allcock and Norman Rand. Before Armstrong bought us, it was total disarray, disorganization, a filthy atmosphere. Nothing like what we have today. That made my job of hiring and firing very difficult. There were days where I hired a guy and that same day the person wouldn't show up."

"How many years have you been doing the hiring and firing?"

"Eighteen years—it was a nightmare!"

"How did you make a quality product?" I ask.

"You couldn't do it. The quality was atrocious. I'm the first one to admit it. You might want to ask Don Richardson, sales coordinator, who deals with the customers. I'm sure he can give you an earful."

"So Don, I'm told that we had high employee turnover in the old days and poor quality."

"It's true!" Don answers. "But only the special valves had quality problems, not our boiler valves. It was difficult keeping the customers happy. Our customers didn't come back. We had to find one big customer, each and every year. Today, we have great quality and short deliveries to our loyal customers."

Just then the phone rings. As Don picks it up, I walk away with a page of notes. This is what it said: 🔥

> *Behind every great company are employees who stay.*

THE MORAL OF THIS STORY

1. Want to improve your quality? Have a stable work force. The longer your people stay with your company, the better the quality of their work. It therefore becomes very important to do everything within your power to decrease employee turnover.

2. Want to improve your customer service? Improve your hiring techniques, attract the best people with good pay and benefits, and provide a climate of trust so they stay.

3. My company can't afford it. You can't afford to have high employee turnover because of the poor quality and poor service that comes with it. Don't forget the additional cost in hiring and training people. Don't forget your customer. How many new customers can you find?

4. If you have morale problems, it could be due to high turnover. When people come and go as quickly as they did for Everlasting Valve in the 1970s, it was difficult for fellow workers to get to know each other. Do *your* fellow workers know each other's *first* name? If they don't, your turnover is too high. If your turnover is high due to retirement, that's acceptable.

Stories
to
inspire
innovation

CHAPTER X

41
A German Accent

Early one morning, a group of people from several countries viewed a new product being demonstrated in our lab. It was beautiful! The product was performing better than anyone had hoped. As they installed the next new product for testing, someone said, "The demonstration room really needs a facelift. It's embarrassing to bring our customers here. We should approach management and ask for money to remodel it."

"I agree. But what can we do? The capital budget has already been approved."

"I know! We can remove some items on the capital budget and use that money." They immediately found $30,000, but they needed more.

Then someone said, "Let's cancel the tooling and pattern investment for the Bypass Trap."

"That won't be popular with management. They've already approved the Bypass Trap and promised it to our joint venture overseas."

"Yes, I know, but I think the demo room is more important than the Bypass Trap. Don't you?"

Later that day, they held a meeting in Ray Masnari's office. The group made a plea to take part of the capital budget and reassign it for the demo room facelift. The only regret was that the Bypass Trap would have to be canceled. Management responded,

"How can we do that? We've promised it to our joint venture overseas."

Suddenly, our German salesman, Jochen Boehike, owner of Technisches Buro in West Germany, spoke in broken English, "Bypass trap? No problem. Just take a stainless steel trap and two test valves. Take the discharge lines on each test valve and attach them together and you have a Bypass Trap." Everyone looked at each other and smiled, "Can it be that simple?"

Jochen said, "I've already done this in Germany. It's no problem; it's working fine." Jochen's German accent was crystal clear; management agreed to reallocate the capital budget to the demo room. The Bypass Trap would be designed as Boehike had explained.

One day later a prototype was built and sent to our friends in Japan. 🔥

> *Ideas become finished acts in a business*
> *which practices urgency.*
> *— Stanley M. Davis, author,* **Future Perfect**

THE MORAL OF THIS STORY

1. Mr. Davis said, "Time should join the ranks of price, quality and service in determining market niches." The Bypass Trap was designed in one day, not three months, thanks to Jochen's idea.

2. Adam Armstrong, my great-grandfather, was a master at quick tries. With these quick tries came mistakes, but also new products. We must go back to that era; the era where my great-grandfather believed in a culture of action, experiments and repeated tries. As Armstrong International, Inc. continues to grow, we slow down the process of innovation. We do this unknowingly because we want to smooth our production flow, protect our turf, try for big home runs, and have procedures which prevent fast tries.

3. New products designed too quickly result in poor quality.
Not true! The reason? Projects under a tight deadline (which move quickly) do not allow enough time for the design engineers to reinvent the wheel. If you do not reinvent the wheel, you must base part of your new design on old technology—old technology which is normally good quality.

4. New products should not solve customers' needs 100 percent—at least, not the first design. We tend to over-design and try to solve the problem 100 percent, which prevents us from trying something *today*. It's okay to have only some questions answered. The time we save makes up for it.

42
Foster Parents

There comes a point with most projects when a "foster parent" is needed — this happens when the original champion leaves the project.

So begins this story.

When Jack Koerwer, an engineer at Everlasting Valve in New Jersey, left his project, he had spent the last year creating a computer software program specially tailored for Everlasting Valve. Now, it just so happens the cost of goods dropped over 10 percent at Everlasting Valve during the first year the new software was in place.

"How could this be?" I wondered. "If we could only do the same at our other divisions."

I caught a flight to Everlasting Valve the next day. While practicing Managing by Storying Around (MBSA) in each of the departments, I eventually told my stories on profits, which led to discussions on the cost-of-goods being so low. Each and every department had favorable comments on the new software.

When I talked to Dick Base, vice president finance, and Bob Bunting, president, they said, "David, we were against this program in the beginning, but the people wanted it. We told them it was okay so long as they got their jobs done and didn't need any money or additional manpower. And look what they did! What's even more interesting is that Jack Koerwer left and Marc Franciosa (engineer) and Ed Miechowicz (draftsman) took over and completed the project. We should mention that Jack still works on Saturdays, even though he's employed at another company."

I went to Marc and Ed and asked why they became foster parents of this project. It wasn't their idea, so why did they nurture it and keep it alive?

Ed enjoyed the challenge of installing Computer Aided Design (CAD) into the software program. This was Ed's motivator. Marc enjoyed working with computers and there were many requests for the new software which needed to be tailored to each department—Marc's motivator.

Through our talks, I also learned they were working Saturdays and Sundays—sometimes quite late—without pay. 🔥

> *The secret to good ideas is using them —*
> *not thinking of them.*

THE MORAL OF THIS STORY

1. You have a smorgasbord of ideas to choose from. Thanks to Jack and other great leaders, there are plenty of good ideas waiting to be used. Your task is to pick which ones will work at your company and use them.

2. This story is not about software, but about using another person's idea. Foster parents like Marc and Ed made this project work. It took Jack to create it, but Ed and Marc had to keep it alive. It's too bad we don't have more foster parents—just think of all the good ideas being wasted.

3. Where in the story did it say "It wasn't invented here." Or "Oh, we tried that once." Or "It's just not us." You didn't read that because good "foster parents" understand it's more important to raise the child (project) than giving life (thinking up the project). Can you be a foster parent?

43
Hot Wheels

I can remember my younger brother, Patrick, playing with Hot Wheels (the toy cars) when he was a young boy. Yesterday, I saw my son, Chad, playing with Hot Wheels, but he was dipping them in cold water and then hot water.

I asked, "Chad, why are you doing that?"

"Watch what happens, Daddy. I can make the cars change color." Each time he did this the car changed color.

I thought to myself, "Here is an old product that has been made to look new by adding a feature that changes the car's color through temperature." I went to Chad's favorite store, TOYS Я US, and purchased 15 Hot Wheels.

I flew to Three Rivers, Michigan, and handed the Hot Wheels out to each of the salespeople.

I said, "I want you to think of new or existing products that could use this temperature-sensitive paint as a feature. Here is your own hot wheel to put on your desk as a reminder to come up with ideas on using this paint."

You should have seen their faces! Their reaction was always the same; one of shock and amazement that I would consider taking a highly engineered product and redesign it by using the features of a toy. Then awareness set in. Maybe it could work.

The next step was engineering. When I approached engineering the story was the same. "David, how can we take an idea from something as simple as a toy and use it on our technically engineered products? They thought to themselves, "Where is the reasoning, the logic and the common sense? How can you even think of such an idea?"

As we discussed the possibilities of using the temperature-sensitive paint, engineering agreed to do a study on the characteristics of the paint. Duane Harback, product engineer, was assigned the task of calling the paint manufacturer to obtain all information available so it could be cross-checked with the needs of the sales department. 🔥

> *Every business owes its birth and life*
> *to an existing and daring idea.*
> — *James Conant, president, Harvard University, 1933-1953*

THE MORAL OF THIS STORY

1. Sometimes the best ideas are simple —not complex. I would love to report that this idea worked. To be honest, it's too early. The object of the story is not to see if this idea works, but to get people comfortable in taking simple ideas and applying them everywhere. Simple ideas can be good ideas; furthermore, no one said engineered products had to be complex.

2. Swiping an idea from a toy manufacturer…Is this possible and usable on a technically engineered product? Yes, creative swiping can come from anywhere if people only keep an open mind.

3. Take an old product and update it with a new feature. If we were to paint our current products we would not need to change expensive tooling, fixtures or molds. We would not manufacture a new product with low unit volume; thus, high cost. We would actually increase the sales of a current line which helps decrease the cost of each unit sold because we have larger production runs to cover the overhead.

44
It's A Small World

$\mathbf{I}$n Italy, the company Cerrutti, manufacturer of printing machines, wanted to improve their product. Cerrutti wanted to automate the steam output to match the width of the paper being printed on their machines. If their printing machine could adjust the amount of steam being used, they would save energy, increase the service life of their machinery and improve the quality of printed paper.

The question was, who to call to help develop this product? The obvious answer was Armstrong International, S.A., located in Liege, Belgium. Jean Marie Faumas, assistant European marketing manager, took the phone call from Cerrutti. At first, Jean Marie did not know how he could satisfy this customer. However, he knew this was the second largest producer of printing machines in the world and he wanted their business. Therefore, he approached Albert Van Vyve, lab manager, to help design a new *adjustable* steam jacketed manifold. Albert helped Jean Marie design the new unit. Then, they approached Salvatore Cimino, tool maker, to help manufacture the prototype parts. As with any new product, the first few prototypes did not work for various reasons. Finally, after six months, they had an acceptable product to sell the customer.

The customer flew to Belgium to see the new adjustable steam manifold, and was very pleased with the unit. Cerrutti was impressed that somebody actually listened to their needs and did something. We received our first order.

Since that time, we have sold over 100 of these units to several customers. As with any new product, the cost of goods was high at first, and today it's acceptable. Since the unit has become a success, drawings have been developed for manufacturing. Other items have been added to the unit to help make it more user friendly: 1) a digital counter to determine how far the width of the steam will flow versus a visual check, and 2) a pneumatic operated motor instead of the original hand-cranked unit. 🔥

> *Global Leadership by Global Innovation.*

THE MORAL OF THIS STORY

1. Global champions have the same passion and love for their ideas. Once again, we see committed champions doing whatever it takes to make a new product. Jean Marie wanted to service a new customer, and Albert wanted to help design a new product in a timely fashion. Salvatore wanted to help by producing the parts, even without drawings. Wow!

2. Global innovation is messy, sloppy—unorganized, designed by the wrong person, for the wrong market, by the wrong division, at the wrong time, and in the wrong place. Believe me! Don't try to organize innovation.

3. Global customers want to be involved in designing new products. Getting the customer involved is important—regardless of the country. Here, we see the customer (Cerrutti) extremely impressed because someone listened to them, so they flew to Belgium to review the product. Cerrutti then placed an order to try it out.

4. Know when to add features. The first thing you must do is get your idea to work by keeping it simple. The first unit was manually cranked. Once it worked, improvements were made; i.e., an air-operated motor was added so cranking could be eliminated.

45
The Bug Terminator

This story is dedicated to Brian Kimbrough, Jim Wonderly, Mike Roberts and Jerry Downey.

Sit back, relax and let your imagination run wild as I tell you a story about *The Bug Terminator*. Bugs, those wonderful, tasty tidbits that line the bellies of frogs, should not be in our food. Yet the reality at many plants in the food processing industry is that bugs are attracted to food. And how can they kill the bugs without using a bug spray or insecticide which contaminates food? What can they do? Who can they turn to?

A call is made to Armstrong-Hunt, Milton, Florida. "We need help. We need to find a way to kill the bugs. Can we use a unit heater?"

Armstrong-Hunt made a unit heater, typically used to heat space in a large factory. By using heavy duty coils (which Armstrong-Hunt is famous for) and increasing the steam pressure, we can increase the heat to over 140 degrees, which kills the bugs. They placed the unit heaters throughout the factory— and the bugs met their doom.

"Several more bug terminators were sold throughout the country." As the salesman from Armstrong-Hunt told this story, "We decided to call the unit heater by a new name. We called it *The Sterilization Unit Heater.* We would have called it *The Bug Terminator* or *The Bug Killer*, but we didn't think those names were appropriate for an Armstrong product."

I asked, "Why not? I would have used The Bug Terminator!" Later I thought, "Maybe the customers wouldn't like that name." 🔥

> *Look out, Raid! Armstrong has a bug killer that has no chemicals.*

THE MORAL OF THIS STORY

1. Arm & Hammer Baking Soda® was once used for cooking. Then we found it being promoted as a toothpaste, the "natural" toothpaste. Now we find it in our refrigerator to absorb odors. Armstrong-Hunt's unit heaters are used to heat buildings. Now they are used to kill bugs. What's next? The point is, finding a new use for an existing product line is *innovation.*

2. Find a new use within our niche. Developing a new product from an idea or finding a new *use* for the product is only part of the battle. Selling it to your customers is another part. Selling *The Bug Terminator* (I still like the name) to our market niche will be much easier than selling it to an industry we do not call on— such as farmers.

3. The Armstrong name is known in the food processing industry—especially when steam is used. By using our name, the customer knows who we are, what we stand for and what our salesmen stand for. But what do we call the product? Brand image is very important. Brand image should be something that stays in your mind, such as *The Bug Terminator.* But be careful with the name you choose. Does it imply something bad? *Sterilization* sounds healthy, whereas *Bug Killer* makes you wonder where the bugs died.

4. Sometimes new uses for products are found outside our niche. This doesn't mean we can't pursue or sell an idea to another company or try to sell it ourselves. It is going to be more difficult to get acceptance in the market, since our sales force is unfamiliar with these users.

46
Executive Toys

Dedicated to: John Abreu, Jim Bundy, Roger Jensen,
          Marc Franciosa, Ed Miechowicz, John Todor,
          Jim Wilson

The plane's wheels squeal as they touch the runway. I'm thinking, "I'm going to have fun today at Everlasting Valve Corporation in New Jersey. The engineers are in for the surprise of their life." Bob Bunting, president, meets me and we head for lunch. We meet up with Dick Base, financial controller, and I say:

"It's important to know how to innovate, but equally important is attitude and the environment your innovators live in."

Bob nods his head in agreement, and Dick smiles with curiosity on his face.

"Let me tell you the idea I have for Everlasting Valve. It begins with a suitcase... "

We finish our lunch.

Back at the office, the engineers start wandering into the conference room where they have a scheduled meeting with me. With notebooks, calculators and pencils in hand, they take their seats. They are followed by the purchasing manager and the manufacturing manager. After Bob welcomes me, he backs up into the corner with Dick Base to watch the surprise unfold.

I say, "Gentlemen, you won't be needing your notepads, pencils or calculators today. So go ahead and put them on the floor. We're going to have a little play time. We're going to do something very different, so please keep an open mind."

The serious look on their faces now becomes more intense. I reach over, pick up my large suitcase, and slowly unzip it... **Zipppp.** I then turn the suitcase upside down and out fall boxes of toy Legos.

"I told you this was going to be different. Here's the rule. I want you to build something in 15 minutes. You cannot ask any questions; the time starts now.

Quickly, each person grabs a box, opens it, and spills the black, blue, yellow and red Legos onto the table. There were toy Lego men, toy Lego boats, toy Lego cannons, big Legos, small Legos, different shaped Legos and Legos with hinges. Oh, I forgot; the instructions also fell onto the table, but all of the engineers used the picture on the box as reference for building.

Each of the Lego builders began to laugh and joke as they completed their project. At the end of 15 minutes everyone had completed a new product. Bob, Dick and I watched each person's characteristics and took notes. You will find our notes in the morals. I left the next day for a new division, suitcase in hand, my plane ticket read "Destination...?" 🔥

> *Building Legos should be a required course in college.*

THE MORAL OF THIS STORY

1. A visionary is never in his/her time. Building Legos with your children in the family room is fun and nonthreatening. Building Legos in the conference room, where you work and where your peers can see you, is scary, uncomfortable, embarrassing, threatening to your self-esteem. We're adults, business people; we can't be seen playing with toys! I believe that deep down almost everyone liked the idea. But to admit it openly and in front of others was too risky. We tried the Legos idea at another division. I must be honest; few liked it and most felt uncomfortable building toy

Legos. They kept closing the door so nobody would see them. What we learned about our engineering groups at each division was worth more than the time spent building Legos, cost of the Legos and the risk I took in introducing this concept to our people. When I purchased the Legos at Toys Я US I couldn't wait to tell the cashier, "I'm buying the Legos for our engineering staff and here's our company credit card." She laughed and asked if I was serious. I replied, "Of course. We've even changed the name to Imagineering."

2. "*Who* asked the question" is just as revealing as "*what* the question was." After the 15 minutes were up, we had a two-hour discussion on what we learned from this play time. Sometimes "who asked the question" was more revealing than "what was asked." For example, Marc Franciosa asked, "Can we work in teams?" This might suggest Marc believes in working as a team.

3. Why Legos? Legos are supposed to be easy to build. After all, they are for children. Developing new engineered products is supposed to be complex and difficult. Wrong! Everything is as simple as you make it. Building Legos was an exercise to convince our engineers how to think and keep things simple when developing engineered products. Jim Wilson finished his project in five minutes, but had more than half the parts still in the box.

4. Why 15 minutes? We only gave 15 minutes because everybody knows putting Legos together doesn't take a long time. It's supposed to be fast, easy and fun. It's been argued by many of our engineers that doing things quickly, with lots of failures and mistakes, produces poor quality; this is not true! The reason is that under tight deadlines, moving quickly with limited resources prevents you from reinventing the wheel. If you're not allowed to reinvent the wheel, you are basing part of your new design on old technology—which is good quality. Large team projects done over a period of time, normally in a long period of time, with unlimited budgets and large staffs, have a tendency to develop new concepts and do try to reinvent the wheel. Thus, the possibility of poor quality. Short deadline equals quality innovation.

5. Kids don't use the instructions; only the adults do. Wrong! In our engineering group at Everlasting Valve, not one of them referred to the instructions. Few did at the other division. Granted, some looked at the box and tried to copy the project quickly. The reason? They knew their deadline did not allow them to follow the detailed blueprints which would have taken closer to an hour. The lesson learned… "Not all prototypes need fancy blueprints or instructions. Sometimes a simple pencil sketch or simply cutting the metal and putting the parts together is all that is required. How could they disagree with this fact when they didn't use the instructions as they assembled their toys?

6. Imagination is only for children. Wrong again! Granted, a lively imagination is found more often in children than adults. But we had a few who dared to dream. Some built a product that did not resemble the picture on the box or in the instructions. They did something completely creative in their mind and transformed it into a Lego part. Imagination was the key thing expressed by these people, so why not express creativity within the business when developing new products? The answer given by John Abreu, "There are too many restrictions!" We then found what those restrictions were, defined them, eliminated some. John said, "This will help me be more creative."

7. We forgot the Tinker Toys! What could we have learned with Tinker Toys? Maybe the person who grabbed them did so because he hates change. Does this same person use the new CAD system or does he stick to the old ways of doing things? If you take the Lego exercise, you can also make some changes to it: Take some pieces out so they're missing from the box; mix the pieces up; change the instructions so they're in the wrong box; put the parts in the wrong box so they don't match the picture. Watch how your people respond. After all, innovation is never a true science. There is always at least one resource missing, such as time, money, manpower, or equipment. Something goes wrong; something gets lost, such as the instructions. It's not fair—but that's the way innovation works. We have to learn to adapt.

8. Clean up the mess. After two hours of discussion, you will find vast amounts of new ideas, change, and chaos becoming apparent. Your people need to be refocused. Ask each of the Lego builders the following questions: "What one thing did you learn from this exercise and how will you use it in your *job* today?" Their answer must only be one, two or three key *words*, such as "teamwork," "keep things simple," "not to perfectionize," "urgency," "creativity." These words will give each person his/her summary of what to practice.

9. "Leaders create the future by emphasizing what the company's people must learn, not by reinforcing what they already know." Harvard Business Review said this and would approve of Legos— I think. Does Harvard have a Lego 101 class? Why not!

47
Silver Bullet

Several years ago, Armstrong-Yoshitake, Michigan invented a new repair part for radiator traps called the "Silver Nugget." (We should have called it the "Silver Bullet".) It was used on radiators at low pressures. This new product was *not* designed in the normal product design process. There were no drawings and very little documentation of lab testing—less than two weeks of life cycle testing was done. Only two people developed the product, Gary Maxam (engineer) and Marv Rinehart (tool & die maker). The Silver Nugget was released into the market. It was a safe product, but they were not 100 percent sure it would last longer than six months. They had no choice; their bosses wanted it and wanted it *now*. What could they do? He wouldn't listen to any excuses. He did ask if it was safe; Gary and Marv answered, "Yes, it's safe." But still they thought, "Why is it so important to have it done so fast?"

Armstrong-Yoshitake asked Armstrong International, Inc., Michigan to manufacture the Silver Nugget. The tool room made the dies and the punch press department blanked the parts and assembled the Silver Nugget.

Due to the way it was developed, several problems arose. **First problem**—the hex design was not deep enough to fit the Allen wrench which installed the Silver Nugget. **Second problem**—some of the gaskets leaked and would not hold the alcohol charge. **Third problem**—the parts did not fall within tolerances.

A meeting was called with all of the departments involved in the project. The defects were discussed to obtain input and ideas for solutions. Prints and dimensions were changed and dies were redone (with extra set-up time in the press department to try these dies). New gaskets were ordered and a sample run was made, which worked well on lab tests.

A short while later, Armstrong-Yoshitake was shipping better quality Silver Nuggets to its customers. 🔥

> *You must be first to the market.*
> *Second means nothing if you want market share.*

THE MORAL OF THIS STORY

1. Fast development results in more mistakes. The good news is that you know which mistakes to fix sooner.

2. Failure is okay if done quickly and if something is learned from it. Armstrong-Yoshitake did not follow standard procedure in designing the Silver Nugget. The imperfections were corrected with two major benefits (by releasing it to the market quickly)— sales of $50,000 and customer input telling us we needed a deeper hex design for installation.

3. When designing a new product, get it to market quickly. Gain experience from the market and make corrections in the design. In short, don't over-design or spend too long fixing every potential problem. If you do you won't get the product to market before competition does. Of course, always remember the core value of providing a safe product.

4. Small beginnings can become big endings. We now use the Silver Nugget in several other products which were never dreamed of. You never know what will sell in the market or how it will be used. Many new products are discovered by accident. The same can be said for the applications they go on. Get to market quickly and let those surprises happen.

Stories to make everyone a *leader*

CHAPTER XI

48
Hoops

Thursday night is known for basketball at Armstrong International, Inc., Michigan. Tonight was no exception as each department prepared for the Armstrong championship. Several departments brought in ringers. Armstrong-Yoshitake invited Steve Masnari since he had played basketball in school.

The game began and Steve immediately took the ball and scored. As they got further into the game, Steve realized his team lacked experience and needed coaching. He gave them hand signals to position them and, when time was available, talked with them.

After the first quarter, the game was tied and Steve began passing the ball to set up plays. Steve could have easily shot the ball in the hoop, but decided to give the others a chance. By the third quarter, Armstrong-Yoshitake was losing by a *large* margin. Steve continued to pass and did not become a ball hog. There were a few times during the game when things got a little heated, but Steve controlled his temper and remained a sportsman. As the clock ticked down, Armstrong-Yoshitake had lost the game.

Steve sat to watch the next game and the person beside him said, "Steve, remember your interview with Armstrong-Yoshitake?"

"Yes, it's next week."

"Well, you just had your interview. Do you want to know how you did?"

Confused, Steve said, "What do you mean, I just had my interview?"

"Well, number one, I can tell you're a team player. You passed the ball, and even under pressure when you could have taken control of the game, you still worked with the other people. This shows you get along with people. Number two, your coaching showed you share your knowledge. You didn't try to 'grandstand' to make yourself a star. Number three, you controlled your temper during a couple of heated moments, which means you won't lose your cool when dealing with customers or fellow workers. Number four, you never gave up, which shows a positive can-do attitude."

"But why did you interview me during a basketball game?"

"I couldn't bring you in for a traditional interview, since you currently work for a headhunter who prepares applicants for interviews. You know all the questions and correct answers. I had to take you out of your environment to check you out. As far as I'm concerned, your behavioral pattern fits the Armstrong culture; we'll check the technical side later."

> *Nature gave us one tongue and two ears*
> *so we could hear twice as much as we speak.*
> — *Edward Pictetus*

THE MORAL OF THIS STORY

1. Look for behavioral patterns. Build "behavior traits" for each job. By "build" I mean list those behavioral traits you currently like about your best employees. Ask questions during the interview to find out if the applicant has these traits. Steve was a team player, good coach (kept his cool) and he had a can-do attitude — traits Armstrong looks for when interviewing.

2. Stories can be used for interviewing. Use your stories on innovation when interviewing engineers. Ask them to tell you if they agree with the morals; or, better yet, have them provide you with the morals (without seeing your morals). See if they match your morals. This will help confirm that the candidate can fit into your company's culture.

3. Think of it as a marriage proposal. Don't rush your interviews. You have to live with your choice for 30-plus years! Some of our interviews have lasted seven years.

49
Lunch With the President

"Gus, thank you for inviting us to lunch. Do I understand correctly that we can ask you any question and you'll answer it?"

"Yes—and if I can't give an answer the reason is that it's for the good of the company."

A lady across the table asked, "Can you tell me why it takes so long for our health care program to send a refund check? Sometimes it takes as long as 30 days before we get it."

Another person agrees, "Yes, and sometimes they don't give us a full refund. They want to know why we had certain tests done, why we stayed at the hospital and why we went to the emergency room."

Gus said, "I was not aware that it took 30 days to receive your refund. I'll look into it." (He pencils down a note.)

"Gus, sometimes the paperwork is so confusing that I have Helen Greene, personnel director, help me fill it out. Why can't they make the form simpler?"

"Yes, that's right. Make it simple!" replies another.

Once again, Gus pencils a note and replies, "We'll look into simplifying the forms. I'm sorry for the inconvenience."

Once a week, Gus Armstrong, president of Armstrong International, Inc., had lunch with 12 employees so he could answer questions. He found a common complaint after several lunches. The health care program was not being perceived as a benefit. It was being perceived as a non-trusting, complex, slow-paying hassle for the employees.

Gus thought to himself, "We're paying a lot of money for this program and we're getting a black eye. I think it's time for a change."

The change soon came in the form of Armstrong's self-insured health program. Since this change, our health insurance costs have gone up considerably, but so have other health insurance plans. Today, Armstrong's health plan is perceived as a Cadillac plan. Refunds are paid more quickly.

One day, Barb Gordon came to me and said, "David, I just want to thank you and the company for all the health care expenses you covered for my husband. The bills were large and I never really appreciated our health care program until I needed it. If there's anything I can do, just let me know."

I replied, "Barb, there is something you can do. Go tell 10 other employees how great our program is. We spend $350 a *month* per *person* and you're right… it is a good plan."

"I'll be happy to do that."

> *You only live once. Take care of yourself.*

THE MORAL OF THIS STORY

1. Health care plans should be a benefit, not a black eye. If your people *perceive* your benefit plan as a hassle and unfair, you've not received the benefit you paid for. **CHANGE IT!**

2. Health care plans should be simple. If it's too complicated to fill out the forms or understand what the program covers, the people will not be happy. **CHANGE IT!**

3. Health care plans are expensive. The only way to reduce costs is to have healthy people or to control expenses through an approval board. If you have an approval board which reduces bills paid, your people will be unhappy. Remember to advise your approval board that their purpose is to provide health insurance, not just to save money.

4. Sick people will cost you more. If you're self-insured, you pay for it that year. If you're insured by a major insurance company, your rates go up the following year. In either case, you pay if your people are ill. Self-insured programs give you more control over the plan and allow you to present it as a benefit to your employees because of the way claims are handled (payment in five days, not 30 days).

5. We reminded our employees to have their spouse go to their employer first and Armstrong second. Sometimes you must remind the employees of the do's and don'ts of your program. Our plan was so good, some spouses who worked for *other* companies used Armstrong's self-insured program first because it was hassle-free and paid quicker. We reminded these people to use their employer first.

50
Spider Webs

The date is September 11, 1991, and I'm visiting Armstrong-Hunt, Florida. I've just walked through the office/shop door and I immediately see a familiar face. "Hi, Chuck. It's been a long time since we've had a chance to talk."

"Hi, Dave. You're right; I think it's been over two years now. How does the place look?"

"It looks real good," I answer.

"It should, especially since we removed all the spider webs from the ceiling just for your visit. Several of us had to climb on ladders and get into the rafters to get the webs. Actually, we really do keep the place quite clean, but we always go that extra mile when someone from Corporate comes to town."

That evening, as I'm driving to the restaurant in the company car, I notice a piece of masking tape (stuck to the chrome on the hood) flopping in the wind. When I arrive, I grab the masking tape and walk into the restaurant. I take my seat and say hello to David Boykin, David Dykstra, Carl Looney, Tony Thompson and then turn to Chuck Rockwell, "Chuck, I found this masking tape on the car. Next time you have the car painted, you might want to make sure all the tape has been removed."

Chuck answers, with a laugh in his voice, "You know, I saw that masking tape while I was driving back from the paint shop, but when I arrived I'd forgotten to remove it."

Everybody at the table begins to laugh.

Chuck continues, "You know, it's been two or three years since that car was last painted and it really needed it!"

"That's interesting, Chuck. That was about the last time I visited Armstrong-Hunt. What do you do — paint the car every time I come to town?"

Everybody begins to laugh even louder.

Then I look across the table and mention, "You know, I was also told that it's nice to see a certain person in the office wearing a tie, and it always happens when I visit." Again, everyone laughs and looks at Carl.

"That's true, David. I do wear a tie when you or others come to town."

"Now that we've had some good laughs, let's talk about products of the future."

Some questions can be asked, but they can't be answered.

THE MORAL OF THIS STORY

1. Questions show interest. If someone brings a project to you and you ask good questions (as their leader), that shows interest — which in turn motivates.

2. Questions take time — a lot of time. Giving up your precious time says, "I really care." If you cannot spend the time (15 minutes) to listen and ask questions, you will be perceived as not *really* interested.

3. Your lead into a question can set the tone. A positive remark followed by your question shows support, i.e., "Your new product is worth millions; what testing have you done?"

4. Questions can take away ownership if asked at the wrong time. If you've delegated a project and set a due date, don't ask the status of the project until *after* that date has passed. Otherwise, it would show a lack of confidence in that person; thus, take away ownership. Let them bring up the due date—they always do. Now you can talk about the due date since they brought it up.

5. Questions can de-motivate or scare people. Be careful about *what* you ask and *how* you ask a question. A smile on your face, a positive tone, a relaxed stance…

6. Not all questions can be answered. If you are a leader and a difficult question is asked and you don't have the answer, don't second-guess your abilities in leadership. If you're the person asking the question and you *don't* get an answer, don't assume the person is hiding something from you. There are some questions that just cannot be answered.

51
The Baton Relay Race

The baton relay race shows the efficiency of teamwork by dividing the effort needed to win between four racers. Let's not forget the number one objective is to be the first team to cross the finish line.

I use this analogy because it illustrates the design and manufacturing that took place on the water heater which is sold by Armstrong-Yoshitake, Michigan. Armstrong International, Inc., Michigan and Armstrong-Hunt, Florida had to assist because Armstrong-Yoshitake had no design engineers or manufacturing engineers.

Customers had placed orders and there was an urgent need for inventory. The timetable to finish the design and produce inventory was nearly impossible. The new water heater was to be one of the most complex products ever manufactured at Armstrong International, Inc., Michigan. The coordination required between the three divisions made communication extremely important. All three divisions committed to a due date. The product champion and team members were in the shop several times every day working on the project. When parts were machined on a rush order they were picked up immediately, not a day later, and taken to the next machine. This immediate attention convinced people there really was an urgent need to complete this project on time. It is impossible to list all of the people involved. The old ways of design and manufacturing would not have met the deadline. Everybody on the team started at the beginning with the same amount of information on the project. Raw material was machined into parts before official purchase orders were sent by purchasing to vendors. Parts were made with unfinished drawings, tooling was ordered before it was known that it was the correct tooling, and machine operators helped make design changes and new software programs to machine the parts. Yes, there was some wasted tooling and material, design errors were made and duplication of efforts did waste time. All of these problems were corrected quickly and inexpensively. The project met its deadline with quality parts in one-half the time normally required. 🔥

> How do you miss a deadline? One day at a time.

THE MORAL OF THIS STORY

1. Produce a sense of ownership when setting deadlines. Tight deadlines were agreed upon by everyone. They were not ordered. It was made clear that no excuses for missing a deadline would be accepted. Whatever it took to hit the deadline was expected. Core values were followed.

2. Remember Aesop's fable, "The Boy Who Cried Wolf"? We as leaders cannot ask for a deadline and then fail to follow up and ask for the product on its due date. If we fail to follow up, the people think we don't care and we are only "crying wolf."

3. Everyone's deadline must be fair. It's not fair for sales and research and development to hold a project for 20 weeks and then turn it over to manufacturing with only five weeks left until the deadline. Share all information from week one. Work together!

52
Total Recall

As the vice president of sales, Armstrong International, Inc. sits at his desk reading reports and mail, his phone rings. He reaches to pick it up, "Doug Bloss speaking."

"Doug, this is Ray Masnari. I'm calling to let you know we are recalling one of the *new* products introduced last month."

Doug leans back in his chair with a concerned look on his face and asks,

"Ray, which product is it?"

"It's the 1-LDC. And wouldn't you know it, we've sold over 500 of them in the first two weeks."

Several seconds pass while nothing is said. Then Doug asks, "Ray, what seems to be the problem with the 1-LDC?"

"It just doesn't meet the quality standards of Armstrong. We thought it did when we introduced it, but we have found that there are some improvements we need to make."

Early that evening, at home, I'm sitting at the kitchen table playing a game of Monopoly with my sons, Chad and Kurt, who are trying to beat me.

As I wait for my turn the phone rings.

"David," Doug said excitedly, "I have an idea on how we can take the recall of the 1-LDC and turn it into a positive event. What if we give one free unit for each unit recalled? All companies have to recall a product on occasion and it leaves a negative feeling. This would help make the people see Armstrong as a first-class company."

"Doug, that's a great idea! I think you're right. This will make Armstrong stand out as a company that cares about the inconvenience the recall has created for its customers."

> *Be patient with the faults of others;*
> *they have to be patient with yours.*

THE MORAL OF THIS STORY

1. Your actions must "smell" like first class. Giving a free product for every one recalled "smells" like first class. Offering a 50 percent discount for the next purchased unit doesn't smell as sweet. Doug understands; if you're going to do it, do it right!

2. How you deliver that "smell" is important. To send the new and free unit without a notice doesn't "smell" as sweet as sending out a thank-you note for their patience, with gold leaf borders and gold lettering. Don't forget to use quality paper. A form letter sours the smell.

3. When you "smell" is important. The "smell" has to be noticed at the right time. You should send your notice immediately upon recall—not one or two months later. Once the people have it in their minds that you have inconvenienced them, there are few things that will change their minds. Make them anticipate and *welcome* the recall. Give them the first-class notice announcing the free unit before their thoughts turn negative.

4. Who "smells?" Take special care to ensure that the proper people "smell." Signing the notice with only your company's name is impersonal. Using everyone's signature in a department—now that has more of a personal touch!

53
Dirty Fingernails

There she stood, attractive, poised, with a smile on her face. She was well dressed with gold jewelry hanging from her wrist and neck. She was clinging to the arm of her husband as they made their journey. Something seemed wrong. She didn't belong in this place. This was not the journey that one would expect to see a woman like her making.

Their journey took them to a person who stood in their path. He was dressed in work clothes with his arms and hands dirty from the day's work. The husband held out his hand in a gesture of friendship. The worker put forth his elbow into the palm of the husband's hand, for his hand was covered with oil and dirt. The husband took the man's elbow from his hand and reached for the dirty hand. After the warm handshake, the hand was pulled back, but to his surprise, the woman held out her hand. Again, the elbow was put forward, and again, the elbow was taken from the hand, as she shook the dirty hand. The journey continued, and each time an elbow was presented it was followed by a handshake from the husband and wife. You've probably guessed, the husband and wife were my father and mother, Gus and Barbara Armstrong, the owners of the company, Armstrong International, S.A. in Herstal, Belgium, which they were visiting for the first time.

Fail to honor people; they fail to honor you.
— *Tzu Lao, philosopher*

THE MORAL OF THIS STORY

1. Reach out and touch someone. What better way than through a handshake? How do you get people to buy into your dream, to give 110 percent, to talk to you, and to care about the company? By your first encounter which begins with a warm, friendly handshake.

2. A great leader shakes dirty hands. Yes, they can wipe them off on a rag or on their pants, but don't feel you can't shake someone's hand because it's dirty. A little soap and water will take care of everything. My father and mother shook many dirty hands that day. This showed they cared and what the people did was important. How many owners or presidents do you know that shake dirty hands? How about their wives? Don't you think it's time for you to become a leader who shakes dirty hands?

3. Shake hands often. Don't do a token gesture, where you only shake the hand once. People will think you are being phony and don't care. We shake hands often in our everyday acquaintances. How many times have you shaken your friend's hand? More than once — right? You should do no less with the people you meet in the shop and office.

4. Here is a secret handshake for my readers. Use both of your hands when you shake hands. One hand in their palm, your other hand on his/her arm. It's warmer, friendlier, and more memorable.

Stories about heroic people

54
The Weekend

Everyone enjoys the weekend. It is a time for being with the family, relaxing and playing. None of us like to give up our weekends for work, whether it's work around the house or overtime at the factory. When asked, we do what we must. That is why the following is so special.

Armstrong International, Inc., Michigan had just purchased a flexible machining center (FMC) made by Gittings & Lewis (G & L) which could run weekends and at night without people. The problem was, the machine needed to be loaded with castings every six to eight hours. The benefits of the machine would be realized only if someone would load it at all hours of the night and on weekends. We don't work weekends.

Before management could ask for volunteers, several individuals offered to come in on the weekend to keep the machine loaded with castings. Mark Henline, John Henline, Larry Haag, Keith Pratt, Brad Kinney and Ed Kirchner were these gentlemen. The FMC has been operating weekends for the past two years, and this has helped Armstrong maintain their vision statement of "service" to its customers.

Opportunities come to those who look for them.

THE MORAL OF THIS STORY

1. The free gift of authority. The only thing you need to do is accept it. These men took authority by offering to come in on weekends.

2. Opportunities must be noticed before you can take advantage of them. You are exposed to several opportunities for improvement every day. Do you notice them? If you do, do you take action?

3. One of the core values of Armstrong is safety, and this was considered when the schedule was arranged. Two people are always in the building at the same time, thus providing safety for each of the workers.

55
Cheapskate?

This story takes place at Everlasting Valve, New Jersey. They were $75,000 behind their original sales forecast. It was going to be difficult to make the $75,000 since they had already shipped and booked every order they could find.

Now enters the hero of our story, MaryAnne Undrosky, who does several jobs: secretary, receptionist, order taker and customer service assistant. Maybe we should even add salesperson.

Management at Everlasting Valve decided to ask for her help. "MaryAnne, in your spare time, would you call customers and try to sell some boiler valves?"

"I would like to, but I don't know who to call."

"That's no problem, MaryAnne. The sales department will give you a list of customers." MaryAnne was given the list of customers and she made calls for the next few days.

Customers began to call Everlasting Valve with their orders. The sales department took the calls and asked, "Can we take your order?" Surprisingly, one customer replied, "No, I want to speak to MaryAnne; she's the one I will give the order to. I want to make sure she gets credit for this sale." At the end of two weeks, MaryAnne had sold $35,000 in boiler valves, which helped Everlasting Valve beat their sales forecast.

Later that month, Everlasting Valve celebrated MaryAnne's success (during a luncheon meeting) with the factory and office workers. They presented her with a $50 bill for her achievements. The managers at Everlasting Valve realized you must celebrate when something special has happened. 🔥

> *Everlasting Valve gave MaryAnne $50.00.*
> *What do you think?*

THE MORAL OF THIS STORY

1. Are we cheap or are we smart? Let me tell you the problems with giving large bonuses. Believe me, we as leaders wish we could give $10,000 bonuses. Here is why we can't:

2. Would you be jealous? Some people would be jealous of $10,000 and ask, "Why don't I get paid for my special contributions?" $50 doesn't create jealousy.

3. Now I can leave the company. $10,000 is enough for some people to quit their job. If $10,000 isn't enough, would $100,000 be enough? We have invested too much time and money in you; we don't want you to leave.

4. How can the company afford to do this every time? Maybe one $10,000 bonus is not so bad, but that amount times 100 or 1,000 people becomes a major expense. This is not a good precedent to set.

5. Will the others think this is a fair bonus? Most of us who have given bonuses know that you cannot please everybody, especially when the bonus is large. You may feel the person receiving the bonus was deserving, but will others? Remember, if they perceive that it is not fair, what problems have you created?

6. MaryAnne might expect $10,000 every time she does something heroic. Worse yet—everybody might start to expect big bonuses for their special efforts.

56
A Four-Leaf Clover

<hr />

Ken Handy had just returned from his family vacation when he turns to his wife and says, "Linda, I'm going to the office for a few hours."

"Okay, but don't work too late. You've had a long day." Ken goes to work and before he knows it the clock strikes midnight.

Several months pass and Ken's name comes up again.

First Worker: "What's Ken Handy doing here? He works in the office; he doesn't work in the shop. Besides, it's Saturday and only the shop is working overtime."

Second Worker: "I don't know why; let's go ask our foreman."

Foreman: "Ken knew we were behind in shipments and he wanted to help out. He's offered to work a full eight hours. What's interesting is that he doesn't get paid overtime because he's salaried."

First Worker: "Did someone ask him to come to work?"

Foreman: "No, from what I'm told, he just volunteered his time."

Time ticks on a few more months when, at lunch, Ken's name comes up again.

"Thanks for coming to lunch, David. I'd like to talk to you about hiring someone for Production Control," says Monty Wood, production control manager. Monty goes into a half-hour detailed presentation to justify the new hire, when finally he says, "By the way, my people have been putting in a lot of overtime. They're starting to burn out."

"Monty, how many hours are they putting in during a week?"

"Sometimes as much as 60 hours."

"Well, we'll have to put a stop to that, but at least they're getting paid time and a half."

"Remember, David, not everybody is on hourly pay; some are salaried."

I think to myself, "Ken Handy is one of those people."

> *I'm a great believer in luck, and I find the harder I work, the more I have of it.*
> — *Thomas Jefferson, Third President, United States*

THE MORAL OF THIS STORY

1. Some people have all the luck! Is it luck when someone is promoted or is it due to heroic effort, like Ken working on Saturday with no pay?

2. He was at the right place and at the right time! Remember, it's a numbers game. The more times you come to work early, leave late, work Saturday, try new ideas, etc., the better your chances of being at the right place at the right time and of being noticed.

3. It's who you know that counts—not how good you are! There's some truth to this; however, it only gives you a chance. You still have to perform. It's like a college degree; it gets you in the door, but you still have to prove yourself to stay employed or get promoted.

4. I'd rather be lucky than good! No, you wouldn't, because if you weren't good, you wouldn't keep your job for long.

L. CONRAD

57
Mrs. Sherlock Holmes

Marcelle Ory is not one of the Armstrong International, S.A. Herstal, Belgium, personnel. She is employed by Ets. Laurenty, a local office maintenance company. Since she started to clean Armstrong's offices, some 10 years ago, she identified herself so well with Armstrong International, Belgium that everybody feels she is a member of the Armstrong team.

Roger Closset, plant manager at Armstrong, said, "It is amazing to find someone so fond of cleaning as Marcelle. Cleaning really means something to her. She performs her job with great professionalism and love. She is concerned with every single detail and nothing escapes her vigilance. She is sometimes called 'Mrs. Sherlock Holmes.' Thanks to her character, we have avoided many problems occurring after our office closing time."

Roger continues to say, "Marcelle works from 16:30 to 21:00. She is interested in everything. She has been taught how to replace the paper roll in the fax machine and to monitor the computer printer after office hours (if something goes wrong, she calls us at home). If someone forgets to turn off a machine, she does it. Recently, a group of 15 important Italian visitors were coming for a seminar to be held in the lab. The lab was left in a disorderly and dirty condition by the workers remodeling it. They were not aware of the Italian visitors coming. Although it was not entirely Marcelle's responsibility, she did a terrific job of getting the lab cleaned by working into the late evening. Thanks to Marcelle's concern, an embarrassing situation was avoided." 🔥

> *There are times when "feeling"*
> *is as important as "knowing."*

THE MORAL OF THIS STORY

1. Our employees should "feel" the Armstrong way. It is really nice to see such devotion to the Company. Marcelle treats Armstrong as if she were an employee (even though she is not). How do you think Armstrong S.A. made her feel like an employee?

2. You cannot be told how to feel. No written policy or job description can explain how to "feel" at Armstrong. Marcelle knew how to feel; she could feel it through the Armstrong people.

3. How do you create that feeling? A thousand little things made up Marcelle's feeling, not the big things that happen a few times a year. If your employees care about the little things, and about new and non-employees (like Marcelle), they notice their importance and also practice the little things. Caring about the little things becomes contagious.

4. How do you convince people that little things are important? Tell them over and over again, give examples, coach, explain why small things are important, tell a story, (yes, tell a story), promote someone for doing a small thing, give a bonus, or as a leader spend a large amount of time on small things.

58
Roger's Story of Heroic People

"**B**elieve it or not, in the year 1982, Belgium's unions declared a strike. The industry park where Armstrong International, Belgium was located, and local companies FN, Cockerill (steel mill), Memorex, Colgate, Burroughs and our neighbour across the street, Danly, had strong unions so they also went on strike." Roger Closset, plant manager for Armstrong, Belgium, takes a drink of coffee and continues his story.

"Back in 1982 we had no problem at all in the beginning of the social movement but after several weeks Armstrong was the only plant working in the Hauts Sarts area. We were, of course, smart enough to have very few cars on the parking lot; most of our people were parking their cars at the Post House Hotel and walking to the plant. I also made many trips to pick up people.

"Nevertheless, our office and factory were invaded one day early in the morning. The group leader was a socialist union leader, a very tough guy. Some employees came to work while the strikers were blocking the office entrance. The people tried to stop them and force them to stay outside but one secretary was so upset that she pushed the men and entered the office. While walking to her place, one tried to make her fall. She immediately reacted by pushing that man aside and went to her place. At that moment, the rough guy came to her, took her typing machine and raised it up, threatening her with it. She was not scared and told him to keep cool and that he had no right to forbid her to work if she so wanted. Then an office employee intervened and everybody cooled down and could finish the day's work. It was for her a question of principle and respect of each individual's freedom. We were, however, told that we would not be allowed to work the next day.

"The next day, all office and shop employees were at work and very soon we were invaded by about 30 people, many of them women, who were the most aggressive. Some of them went directly to a secretary, accusing her of being on the employer's side and trying to convince her to fight against the employers. She, of course, exposed her own arguments and ideas, and after a while the group left the office rather mad. She reported that she never thought that human beings could express so much violence, aggressiveness and hate as she saw in the eyes of those women while talking to her against the bosses.

After many talks and personal contacts with the mayor of the town (a friend of mine, although socialist) and with the State Policy, we decided to stop working for security reasons. Only management people were allowed to stay at work. I had about 10 managers in the office during that period! The strike was at its height and the employees were really afraid (not all of them) because of what they could read in the newspaper and see on the TV news.

"The next day when I came to work at 6:00 a.m., the entrance was blocked by a few cars and the strikers were across the street. I drove through the yard and parked my car as I normally do in front of the office. No other car was on the parking lot.

I put the lights on in all offices, and started the computer. It was, of course, absolutely quiet. Suddenly, I heard some noise coming from the shop. I was surprised, but also afraid. I still had in mind that years ago the building next to Armstrong burned completely overnight, while being occupied by employees who were on strike.

"When I pushed the door to the shop, I was really surprised to hear the noise from machines. There were four people at work: our maintenance technician, a machine operator, a trap assembler, and a humidifier assembler.

"They told me that they could not accept to be fired by outside people and that if some had the right to strike, they had the right to work. They arrived at 3:00 a.m. with one car. They parked far away from the factory on one small road, put the car on jacks, removed one wheel and installed the legal red triangle. They crossed the field and entered the plant through the back door. They left at 11:00 a.m. in the same way. The other people who didn't act in the same way didn't lose any money since they worked extra time to recoup the hours they were forced to lose.

"Although we were disorganized during a couple of days, we *never lost* one hour of production because of a strike. It is still true today after almost 25 years. To understand the context of this story, one should be aware of the strength of the unions and of the social climate in Belgium. Laws are created almost to force people to be unionized. For example: In the metal industries, the employers have to pay one social contribution to one solidarity fund whose goal is to pay additional indemnity in case of long period of sickness. For unionized people, they get their money through their unions. For the others, they get their money from the fund after a deduction of 15 percent *for administrative cost*.

We once had the same case with one of our non-unionized shop workers and we paid the 15 percent difference.

"In case of unemployment, it is well known by everybody that you get your social security money very fast through unions. This creates support for the unions.

"For the others, it is more complicated since they have to go through a public office and this can take quite a while.

"This is the reason why we at Armstrong have decided to quickly pay our non-unionized workers for unemployment and we recover the money from them after they are paid from the public office.

"That's Armstrong International, S.A.!" 🔥

You're only as good as the people you hire.
— Ray Kroc, McDonald's founder

THE MORAL OF THIS STORY

1. All countries have fair, honest, hard-working people. You just have to find them. Too many times I hear other companies say, "Don't worry about that country. The people are lazy, uneducated, and they can't build a quality product." It's not true; don't you believe them!

2. In the middle of difficulty lies opportunity—Albert Einstein. What opportunity did the employees get? The chance to show how much they cared about Armstrong. We won't forget!

3. No noble thing can be done without risk. The risk these people took makes their story even more memorable and noble. Few people would face this kind of danger to do what is right— but then again, they are not Armstrongers!

> Authored by:
> Roger Closset, Director
> Armstrong International, Belgium
> and David M. Armstrong

Stories
that make a
policy manual
obsolete

59
Blondes Have More Fun—
It's Really True!

It was a dark and quiet room. As I entered the room, the lights suddenly came on. There, in front of me and around the table, stood 12 women with smiles on their faces. Immediately behind them, I saw a bright blue check mark on the wall. I then noticed blue check marks on the napkins, cups and paper plates. This was the beginning of my luncheon meeting, a tradition started by my father (see story "Lunch With The President").

As I seated myself, they asked in unison, **"What does the check mark mean?"**

"I can't tell you until someone figures it out," I replied.

As we ate a wonderful lunch, we talked about various things within the company.

As the final minutes ticked toward the closing of our luncheon, I heard one of the ladies with blonde hair say, "David, do you know what a blonde is doing when she has her hands in the air and is grabbing at air?"

"No."

"She's collecting her thoughts." All the ladies laughed.

Another blonde in the group said, "David, how do you know when a blonde has been working on your computer?"

I shrugged my shoulders and said, "I don't know."

"When you find Whiteout on the screen."

A third lady said, "David, why did the blonde jump over the glass wall?" I paused, then she responded, "To see what was on the other side."

Everybody laughed again. The jokes continued for about five more minutes before we broke to go back to work. 🔥

These morals provide guidelines for age, racial, religious and sexual discrimination.

THE MORAL OF THIS STORY

1. Were these blonde jokes considered as sexual harassment? I think not, since they were told to me by women (some of whom were blondes) with laughter in their voices. However, let's be careful of our fun, for one day someone may take these jokes seriously.

2. Do come forward if you're sexually harassed. We will keep it confidential!

3. If you're a victim or you know someone who has been sexually harassed, you may complain to anyone of authority (someone you're comfortable with). You are *not* required to complain to your supervisor first, especially if said supervisor is the one sexually harassing you!

4. Our investigation will be thorough and prompt. *All* results from the investigation will be kept confidential. This investigation is *optional* and will not be pursued against the wishes of the alleged victim.

5. We will take immediate and appropriate corrective action to stop the harassment once and for all — if you agree. A second option could be to provide general training on acts of harassment or discrimination. For example, this story could be circulated and posted, followed up by training if you were sexually harassed. This choice gives the victim a feeling of safety, since the harasser is not singled out. If the victim *rejects* the company's offer of assistance, a memo stating this will be placed in the victim's personnel file.

6. We will follow up one month and one year later—to be sure the harassment has stopped. We will also check to see if any retaliation has occurred.

7. To do nothing is not an option. Harassment of *any* kind involves the entire company, not just a few.

60
Promotions for Cheaters

Armstrong-Yoshitake was established in the year 1986. The company's basic product was a line of pressure reducing valves. These are products similar to steam traps—but are not steam traps. They also had a sideline of radiator traps. It became apparent that replacement parts were needed for radiator traps, and since Armstrong-Yoshitake did not have manufacturing or engineering personnel the question was raised, "How could they develop repair parts for radiator traps without engineers?"

Armstrong-Yoshitake decided to ask Armstrong International, Inc., Michigan to develop this product because Armstrong has an engineering department. Due to time restraints and a heavy schedule, Armstrong-Yoshitake did not ask for Engineering's help, but approached Marv Rinehart, Tool and Die Maker for Armstrong.

Marv said, "Give me a few days to work on it and I'll have something for you."

"You'll need more than a few days!"

"No, I don't think so; I already have some ideas," answered Marv.

"Do you need any money or help?"

"No, I'll find some material somewhere and work in between projects and at night." In other words he *cheated* and hid his time and expenses under another project. He also worked on his own time.

A few days later Marv had a prototype made out of stainless steel, but he had no drawings, which was not the normal procedure. Marv *cheated* normal procedures by not having drawings made. He did have some rough sketches—really rough.

It was time to test it in the lab. Gary Maxim, mechanical engineer for Armstrong International, Inc., Michigan enters the story at this point. Gary's job was to test the prototype with lab technicians and help design further improvements.

Gary and Marv worked for several months improving the original prototype. They broke several rules. Many people at Armstrong became involved in preparing it for production. Armstrong-Yoshitake introduced the new radiator trap repair part to the market.

Later that year, Armstrong promoted Marv—even though he broke many rules.

> *Honor thy cheater.*
> *— Tom Peters, business writer*

THE MORAL OF THIS STORY

1. Promoting somebody who has creatively cheated the system sends a loud message to everyone. It can be beneficial to your future to "cheat." Find ways to get things done in spite of the system!

2. Honor "cheating." This does not mean honor those who break core values, perform immoral or illegal actions, or function in conflict with the company's strategy for success. If the system has obstacles (procedure manuals, policy manuals and forms to be signed in triplicate) and prevents you from accomplishing something, you may want to creatively cheat the system and bypass these structures—they prevent urgency.

3. Have you forgotten what got you to the top... cheating? Why is it once someone makes it to the top of management they don't let others practice cheating? If it worked for you, it will work for them.

61
Two Policies on the Same Topic—Why?

Etta Griffin puts on her coat, reaches for her purse and heads out for lunch. As she approaches the door leading to the parking lot, she waits in line.

Someone in line turns to Etta and says, "I wonder why we have to wait until noon before we can get into our cars and go to lunch."

"I'm sure there's a good reason for this policy. What I don't understand is why the office people get to leave at 11:55 a.m. Why don't they have to wait by the door?"

My brother, Pat Armstrong, overheard this conversation, and he also wondered why.

That night, over dinner, Pat asked me, "Why can the office people leave at 11:55 a.m. and those in the shop have to wait until noon? That doesn't seem fair to me, does it to you?"

"Pat, I know there's a good reason why we have this policy. I just can't think of it right now. Maybe the shop people need time to wash their hands."

After dinner, that entire night, I tried to remember why.

Finally, the next day, I remembered the reason for the policy. "Pat, several years ago, Howard Lambertson, who was president, started this policy due to the traffic jam at lunch. When Armstrong International Inc., Michigan and Continental Can let out for lunch, a traffic jam occurred. Howard decided to let the office leave five minutes early to beat the traffic. This was going to alleviate the traffic jam.

The second reason he created the policy was for safety. There were no traffic lights on the corner of Hoffman and Highway 131, or at Hoffman and West Main Street. He was afraid that one day somebody would take a foolish chance, cut across traffic and be killed."

"But, David," Pat said, "What about the question of fairness? Is it fair that office personnel leave five minutes earlier than the shop people?"

"Pat, the office people were allowed to leave early because their parking lot is located across Hoffman Street, which is a busy street. The shop's parking lot is behind the building and safe from traffic."

I commented further, "By the way, the office people are required to return five minutes before 1:00 p.m." 🔥

> *Maybe the only good policy is one on safety.*

THE MORAL OF THIS STORY

1. **Policies for safety.** Because of traffic jams and people taking unnecessary risks to cross busy intersections, this policy was implemented. You can never have enough policies on safety.

2. **Policies should change with the times.** We now have a traffic light at Hoffman and Highway 131. We still have no traffic light at Hoffman and West Main Street. Continental Can no longer exists, but General Motors moved into their building. If another traffic light is added and General Motors leaves, we will probably abolish this policy. We should only keep policies that are needed.

3. Policies should be explained to new employees. Etta Griffin was employed after the policy was started and was never told why it existed. *Everyone* must tell new employees about our policies and why we have them. By explaining to others, you also will remind yourself. We all forget in time. I did.

4. Policies should be challenged if you want them changed. Pat did not know why this policy existed. He also thought it was unfair. He wanted to know why. The answers he heard were fair and necessary; thus, the policy was not changed.

62
Armstrong's College Scholarship Program

The times are really good, orders are skyrocketing, production is working overtime, and unemployment across the country is reaching all-time lows. Here we sit in the best of times looking to expand our business and maintain our customer responsiveness. To do so, we need more people. The college student program that has been in effect at Armstrong for over 30 years allows us to obtain much needed manpower on a short-term basis. Each and every college-age son or daughter of an Armstrong employee is eligible to work at the company during the summer, providing them with a real work environment and an opportunity to earn money.

Recently we had the opportunity to benefit from this program. Carl Cummings, who was employed in the Tool Room for 13 years, heard about the need we had in our Production Control Department. His son, Rex, graduated from Western Michigan University and has been working the past seven years for Nippondenso.

Carl talked with Monty Wood, manager of the Production Control Department, about the requirements of the job. Monty remembers Carl's son, Rex, working four summers as a college student in the Production Control Department doing cycle counting. Rex displayed a strong work ethic, he was energetic, and a real people person. Now Rex has the educational background, he has work experience, and he knows the Armstrong organization: Just what we need! Thus, the beginning of a full-time position with the company from which his father recently retired. 🔥

You reap what you sow.

THE MORAL OF THIS STORY

1. A true benefit for an employee also benefits his entire family. Exposure at an early stage in life at Armstrong helps instill a good work ethic. It also reinforces financial support. College-bound students in the last few weeks of their classes ultimately begin thinking of how they are going to spend their summer. Needless to say... making money to help pay for college tuition, room and board, books, new clothes, and transportation are all items toward which they know they will have to make a contribution.

2. A true benefit for the company also provides an additional work force. Students are assigned work locations by management. These are areas where the company has the greatest need for additional manpower. These locations might include the machine shop, various assembly areas, drafting, the office, or landscaping.

3. Armstrong pays its first-year students $7.00 an hour... plus a 25 cent increase each and every year the student returns up to four years. Students who work in production on second shift receive an additional 50 cents per hour night premium. Students do not participate in production or year-end bonus programs, nor do they participate in the Blood Bank or receive pay for holidays. Sick days will not be paid by Armstrong.

4. There is more to our college program than making $7.00 an hour. Each of the students also gains experience which makes them more employable. Also they learn what it is like to work on certain jobs so they can decide what career to pursue.

5. Each applicant will be reviewed by the general manager's office. Students are then expected to work 40 hours each week unless prior provisions have been approved by the general manager. At the completion of the summer a review process with the supervisor for whom the student has worked, along with the general manager, takes place to determine if the student is eligible to return for Christmas Break and Spring Break.

6. Armstrong's rules are to be followed. No smoking in office or shop, honor systems such as filling out time cards, paying for food and drinks, and self-inspection for quality also applies.

Authored by:
Rex Cheskaty, General Manager-1995
Armstrong International, Inc., Michigan
and David M. Armstrong

63
Backache

Have you heard the story about Bob Kirchner's sore back? It all begins in the spring of 1995. Bob, commonly referred to as "Tater," works in the Punch Press Department at Armstrong Machine Works in Three Rivers, Michigan. It had been a very busy year for the Punch Press Department. One day Bob was helping Bill Hartman (foreman) move a heavy die.

"Ouch," said Bob.

"What's wrong, Tater?"

"I hurt my back."

"Do you want me to take you to the doctor?" asked Bill.

"No, I've done this before. I know what to do."

This is where the story gets good. Bob Kirchner left work and went to a chiropractor, returning within the hour. The charge for the chiropractor was $20, which Bob submitted for reimbursement through Armstrong's worker's comp.

A few days pass. Bob was told, "We can't cover your bill because worker's comp requires you to see a physician first, and a chiropractor is not acceptable. If you had gone to the emergency room, and seen a doctor, worker's comp would have covered your bills."

Bob replies, "I know that, but all the emergency room would have done would be to give me a few muscle relaxers and charge me over $100. They would also have told me to go home for several days. I was trying to save the company money and get back to work."

"We feel real bad that you're not being reimbursed the $20. Unfortunately, it is a policy that we must follow. Maybe we could find a way to reimburse you."

Bob replies, "No, I don't want any special treatment. I'll pay the $20." 🔥

> *Set the policies to keep your honest people honest.*
> — *Phil Sendell, golfing friend*

THE MORAL OF THIS STORY

1. When policies fail, try thinking. Bob knew that worker's comp would reimburse him for the doctor's fee and hospital emergency room charges. Bob also knew that he would probably get a few days of vacation under the guise of worker's comp. Bob thought about this and decided that it would hurt the company by slower deliveries, paying his salary for no work done, and high medical expenses. The policy fails in this story, but through Bob's thinking, we have a stronger company.

2. No policy covers all situations. The "spirit" behind the reimbursement for medical expenses is not to nickel and dime our people. The "spirit" is to provide coverage for *major* medical expenses that would wipe out a person's life savings. For Armstrong to be able to provide this major medical coverage, we need help. We ask our employees to help share in the expense by paying a yearly premium and a 20% co-payment. Unfortunately, sometimes you hear a story like the one you just read, and you wonder if the policy is fair. Ask someone who has had *major* medical expenses at Armstrong what they think. They will probably tell you how grateful they are.

3. What's in it for me, you might ask? Helping Armstrong keep major medical coverage for you should be enough, but if not, how about this? Bob couldn't help himself. He had to act the way he did in saving the company money because he was brought up that way. Bob's parents taught him to be fair and put in a hard day's work. You've heard the saying, "The cream rises to the top." Armstrong's better employees receive better wages, receive promotions, and are the last to suffer during bad economic times.

Stories
about finding

new sources of

profit

64
Lettuce

"Good morning, Dick! I have to tell you a story I heard on the news last night. It's great! The news came on and the newscaster announced that airlines were going to show losses for the quarter. However, one major airline decided they were going to cut costs. They decided to take the lettuce, which is used for decoration purposes, off the dinner plates. By doing this, they could save $1.5 million per year."

Dick Base, vice president, Finance for Everlasting Valve Corporation, New Jersey, and I laughed at the simplicity and sure genius of the idea.

Then Dick told his story. "At one time, Everlasting Valve also had lettuce. But we called it 'Customer Acknowledgments.' Whenever we got an order, we sent an acknowledgment to the customer. We decided to stop sending acknowledgments because we often shipped the product before our customer received the acknowledgment. There have been few complaints, and we've saved a lot of money by doing away with the lettuce at Everlasting Valve." 🔥

1,000,000 acknowledgments X $.29 postage = $290,000.

THE MORAL OF THIS STORY

1. Why do we have acknowledgments? The answer is: The customer has a lack of confidence in the supplier's ability to meet promised delivery dates, so they want it in writing. The customer also wants reassurance that their order was not lost in the mail or entered into the system incorrectly. Acknowledgments offer a false sense of comfort; mistakes still happen.

2. Build good partnerships with your vendors. Partnerships, not acknowledgments, will provide on-time delivery, accuracy of the order and peace of mind. If you don't have any partners that's okay; you know from *past* performance which vendors let you down. You don't need to ask for acknowledgments, but *if you must*, use them properly.

3. Most customers receive their acknowledgment and don't read it...so why send one? If we send *stock* items before the acknowledgment is received, why send one? If the customer is only checking delivery dates, why send one? Acknowledgments only have value when used *properly*.

4. Only do what has value added. If nothing else, this story makes you think and question why we use acknowledgments. Maybe we should have the computer send acknowledgments by fax. This would save in the cost of forms, filing, handling, bursting the forms, etc. It also would be faster. Can you find other *non-value* procedures (like the acknowledgments) to eliminate?

5. Acknowledgments may play an important role in establishing that the offer to purchase is accepted with *our* standard terms and conditions, not those of the buyer's purchase order (which may be undesirable to us). Before eliminating the acknowledgment, consider how important this factor is in the particular type of transaction. If you're faxing an acknowledgment, consider faxing your terms.

6. How will the customer's receiving department check orders without acknowledgments? They should use their purchase order; they know it's correct because their company wrote it!

7. What do you do if a customer requests an acknowledgment... and you've done away with your acknowledgment forms? You could use your invoice or shop work order and simply write "ACKNOWLEDGMENT" across the top. If you feel *writing* the word appears unprofessional, purchase an "ACKNOWL-EDGMENT" stamp for $5.00 and stamp it.

65
Mother Earth

"**D**ear David," the letter reads, "greetings from the Press Room, Armstrong International, Inc., Michigan. With continued emphasis on cost reduction and savings, we thought we would write to inform you on what we are doing to save money in the print shop and UPS area."

"We are recycling reusable materials as one key to cost savings. Paper clips and literature boxes with the Armstrong logo are reused. We have also informed our workers that Styrofoam packing and popcorn which they receive from incoming boxes should be sent to us for reuse. We have not had to use or order any new bags in over one year. We also devised a rod that sits on the top of the packaging tape machine which allows us to use a roll of tape to the end. We now use every last inch of tape. We turn lights off in the basement, and have advised people who are shipping UPS next-day air into areas that are next day by normal ground delivery not to do so. This also helps keep UPS costs down."

"Finally, we are turning scrap computer paper into note pads. Clean computer sheets are cut, and run through the press to add the Armstrong logo, resulting in a very nice looking note pad. Fax pads are cut to three different sizes to save time and costs on phone bills. We are now *recycling* 12 cubic yards of corrugated cardboard and office grade paper each week, or about 40 percent of our total generated waste. We are also *using* recycled paper which saves more for the environment than it does on the expense account, but it gives us a much finer, more expensive looking paper for about the same price as an ordinary paper."

Respectfully,

Joe D. Wheeler & Janet Blasius

> *What's better than recycling?—Reusing!*
> — *Joe Wheeler*

THE MORAL OF THIS STORY

1. Environmental concerns affect everyone. Pay now or pay *more* later. Businesses will pay great sums of money to meet environmental codes this year. This cost will continue to increase unless we solve these problems today. Everyone has to help save Mother Earth; it's the price of doing business.

2. Eventful concerns set their own priority. We, as leaders, have undeniable obligations to address these eventful concerns (recycling). You do not have the right as a leader to give a low priority to these concerns so you can avoid them.

3. No item is too small to save money on—even paper clips. Joe and Janet understand the importance of saving money on small items. This kind of attitude will help strengthen our company financially.

4. How do you know if your people are trying to save money? Letters such as this one show a deep concern for the environment and on cutting costs. Look for the simple actions such as paper clips piled on a manager's desk, the saving of a single postage stamp when a letter is hand delivered during a business trip, and reports with a routing list to cut down on the number of copies made before mailing.

66
The Herbie Hunt

The book slides across my desk and Steve Gibson, CFO and Vice President of Finance, Armstrong International, Inc. says, "This book's great; I think you should read it. It talks about all the problems in manufacturing and it's done as a novel so it is not so boring."

I look at the title, *The Goal*.

Days pass, "Steve, you were right, the book's great! I now understand manufacturing better than ever. What do you think about having a Herbie Hunt? We both know we have too much inventory and maybe we can find those Herbies that are causing it." To know what a Herbie Hunt is, you must read *The Goal*.

"Sounds like a good idea; let me know when."

August 20, 1990, marked the first day of the Herbie Hunt. We began our search in the Screw Machine Department with Gary Vedmore, the foreman.

"Gary, we're here searching for Herbies," I said.

"What's a Herbie?"

"A Herbie is anything that inhibits production. It can be a machine where orders are backed up, a department which needs more labor to keep up, a machine that breaks down or time spent running inventory and not orders."

"Well, David, I can tell you we run as efficiently as possible." (I know, I just let you check by telling you what a Herbie was.

You should still read the book.)

"Well, David, I can tell you we run as efficiently as possible."

I smiled. "If that's the case, why do you have so many trays of inventory in front of your machines?"

"Those trays are work in process waiting to be put on the machines."

Steve: "Why can't you put them on the machines?"

Gary: "Well, they're backed up and we're already running two 12-hour shifts."

Steve: "Maybe your machines are Herbies. Are you running too many parts across one machine which could be run in another department that has more time? Maybe you need to remove those products with slow sales volume from your machines. Are you scrapping parts, thus losing time because your bar stock is not good quality or can you delete operations to speed up the machining time or setup time?" 🔥

> ### *Work on shipments for today;*
> ### *don't build inventory for tomorrow.*

THE MORAL OF THIS STORY

1. *The Goal* **clearly states:** Reduce inventory and operational expenses while *simultaneously* increasing shipments. If you can't ship it — don't build it! (The goal is not to improve just *one* of the three, but all three together.)

2. Should a machine sit idle? Yes, if you have no orders. Machining parts to keep the machine running does not increase shipments, but increases the work in progress (WIP), thus raising your inventory. How? Purchasing must order more raw materials which you use to keep the machine running. A shortage of manpower is also created by having someone committed to running parts. Therefore, there are no savings in keeping the machine running; you're only wasting inventory and manpower on parts you can't ship.

3. What if it takes 12 hours to set up the machine—and you only have three hours of orders to run? Wouldn't it be better to have a long production run for several days to maximize your efficiency since the cost of setting up the machine is high? Once again, no, unless you have orders to ship. The machine has already been paid for and our labor force is a fixed expense (Armstrong International, Inc. will seldom lay off its people), so where are the savings? A dedicated machine would be better. By leaving it set up, we could only run the parts we wanted to ship and not feel we wasted time setting it up.

4. Leaders must give the tools to obtain the goal. Armstrong is buying flexible, unmanned machining centers so we can have short production runs and not feel wasteful since the setups are short.

5. Answer these three questions when in doubt. Did shipments go up? Did operational expenses go down? Did inventory go down? If you can say yes to these questions, you have obtained your goal: Continuous improvement and profit!

67
Volunteer Vacation

Have you heard the story of Warrick Controls' Volunteer Vacation Program? During slow times, due to poor economic conditions or to the seasonal nature of the product line, Warrick offers volunteer vacation time. Instead of laying people off, a notice is put up asking for volunteers who will take vacation without pay. The response to this has been better than one might think. It seems quite a few parents find it appealing, especially during summer months when they can spend time with their children on vacation before school starts. Sometimes it's just to have a longer vacation than they have available based on years of service. 🔥

> *It's more profitable to keep valued employees*
> *than to find new valued employees.*

THE MORAL OF THIS STORY

1. **Volunteer vacations reduce costs in wages...** just like layoffs, except for one important fact:

2. **Volunteer vacations allow you to keep your employees.** You don't want to lose your experienced workers. Volunteer

vacations allow you to keep them when a layoff would force you to lose them, and because they're voluntary, they're perceived as a benefit by the worker.

3. Volunteer vacation time does not reduce an employee's normal vacation. Volunteering during slow times for the company may not be ideal vacation timing for the employee. The employees have to know their standard vacation time where they may have a routine from year to year, such as Christmas vacation, will not be affected. There can be no exceptions to this rule or they will never trust the company enough to volunteer.

4. Volunteers must be accepted by management. Not all departments are slow when the company is slow. Management must reserve the right to *approve* any volunteer vacations.

5. Volunteer vacations must not be less than one day, and notice must be given in advance. In order to properly plan workload, these guidelines must be followed. Each division has the right to ask for *more* notice and/or more than one day off at a time if they so choose.

6. Benefits will be paid but not wages. We must provide health care and other related benefits or no one can take the risk of volunteering for fear of getting sick. There will be no wages paid for volunteer vacations.

7. First come, first served, provided you are not needed. Trying to apply fairness to this policy will be difficult when you have more people volunteering than you can afford to let go. In those cases, we will choose those who have less work and then those who ask *first*.

68
Everlasting Wooden Boxes

There's a story told about a salesman who had just begun his career at Everlasting Valve Corporation, New Jersey. After spending several weeks in the factory, he decided it was time to visit some customers.

"Good morning," said the customer.

"It's nice to meet you," replied the salesman. "If you don't mind, I thought it would be helpful if I had a chance to see how you install our boiler valves, how you service them, how you receive them from Everlasting Valve, and how you inventory them so I can better service you in the future."

"That's a great idea," said the customer. "Come on, I'll take you on the nickel tour." (It was a long time ago.)

When they reached the factory, the salesman noticed a crane lifting a wooden box slowly into the air. Suddenly, the wooden box fell to the ground with a mighty c-r-a-s-h! Wood splinters flew everywhere and the product came to rest on the cement floor.

"Look out!" screamed the salesman. "Is everybody OK?"

The customer calmly answered, "Everyone's fine. We do this on purpose. The wooden box is built so well that we find it easier to open the wooden box by dropping it to the floor. It takes a lot less time."

The salesman looks down at the floor and sees the name on one of the broken wooden boards. It reads, *Everlasting Valve.* 🔥

> *Money is like promises—easier made than kept.*
> *— Josh Billings, writer and auctioneer*

THE MORAL OF THIS STORY

1. $80,000 was the cost for these wooden boxes. This may not seem like much, but in the 1960s this represented 10% of the total *sales* for Everlasting Valve. It was an unbelievably large cost for which the customer received no benefit. As a matter of fact, the customers found it to be a problem because the boxes were put together so well. The cost of the labor to open the wooden boxes was too high, requiring a customer to smash them on the floor.

2. The wooden boxes were replaced by skids. The savings to Everlasting Valve were simply too large. The customer now saves labor when unpacking our Everlasting Boiler Valves.

3. Packaging can save you money. We must look for cost savings in *all* areas of business, not just in the product. Improvements in accounts receivable, warranties, literature, drawings, and reducing paperwork, all of these put profits into the bank. Remember to look at common sights which normally go unnoticed. Some of the best cost savings are hiding out in the open.

69

"A Penny Saved is a Penny Earned"

One might think this story begins with Ben Franklin in the 1700s, but it does not. The year was 1994, and it is about Tom Stokes, machinist, who works at Armstrong International, Inc., Michigan. Tom works during the second shift on a machine called a Warner Swasey. The Warner Swasey stands five feet high and is eight feet long. In the front are two sliding doors that help protect Tom from the metal shavings as it cuts metal. The door also keeps the fluids used to cut the metal in the machine and from splattering on the floor. It's an older machine in need of some repair, but still does the job.

One night I was in the plant handing out a story to Brad Neumueller. I heard my name paged over the intercom. I recognized the voice as that of Lester Newbre, night foreman. I found Lester and asked him why he had paged me.

"Come on, let me take you over to see Tom Stokes. He's got a story for you." We walked over to where Tom was working.

"Hi, Tom. I hear you have a good story for me." Tom takes off his gloves. We shake hands.

"Yes, I do," he says, as a big smile comes across his face. The other machinist, Terry Reber (behind him) stops to listen. "See the doors on this Warner Swasey?" Tom points to them.

"Well, they're loose, and if they don't fit real tight when you close the doors, the machine won't run because of the safety switch that needs to be triggered. Instead of having maintenance come over and spend a lot of time fixing it, and spending a lot of money, I took a copper penny and used it as a shim."

He points to the penny which is nicely positioned, holding the door firmly in place.

"Now the machine runs great. The solution is, without a doubt, safe and effective."

"That's great, Tom. That shows a lot of imagination in fixing a major problem. You saved the company a lot of money. This is exactly the kind of behavior I'm looking for from Armstrongers. You can bet I'm going to write your story." 🔥

> *Money is of no value; it cannot spend itself.*
> *It all depends on the skill of the spender.*
> — *Ralph Waldo Emerson, poet*

THE MORAL OF THIS STORY

1. A penny saved is a penny earned… in this case it's probably saving us more than a penny. I'm sure it's thousands of dollars. Imagination is a powerful weapon to control costs. Truly, I say to you, these little acts of creativity are how we save money.

2. Tom invested a penny in his machine… and another… and another. You see, every time Tom opens the door where the safety switch is located, the penny falls into the machine and exits where all of the scrap shavings fall. Sometimes he's lucky enough to catch the penny, but not always. This requires another investment of a penny to keep the machine running. The Warner Swasey needs to be fixed. Next time I see Tom, I'm going to give him a roll of pennies to keep it running. How's that for imagination? We won't even need to change the maintenance budget.

3. This penny means more to me than a professionally drafted resume. Most resumes I read are boring. This story reveals Tom's imagination. In my office sits a gum ball machine which I fill with M & M's to remind visitors of the M & M story. The only problem with this gum ball machine was that it required coins to receive the M & M's. One day, Rex Cheskaty (general manager of Armstrong Machine Works) saw me working on it as I was trying to disassemble the mechanism requiring coins to allow the candy to fall into the hands of the hungry visitor. After studying the mechanical device, Rex took a penny out of his pocket and placed it between the spring so no money would be required to operate the unit. His idea was creative and simple. It looks like Tom Stokes has what it takes to become a general manager, don't you think?

4. Imagination is at the heart of our future successes. We depend on creativity to soar to higher heights; without it, we cannot grow in the manner we desire. Besides, it's *fun* to be creative.

Stories about why small is beautiful

70
286-7175

<hr>

The numbers "2-8-6-7-1-7-5" are dialed on our phone. Ringgggggg… ringggg… on the third ring you hear, "Good morning, Armstrong International," Linda Demeritt, receptionist, for our Stuart, Florida, office answers the phone.

"Linda, it's David. Let me speak to Valerie (Valerie Casterline, my assistant)."

"Just one minute, David."

A few moments pass.

Click. "Hi, David. How's your trip going?"

"Real good, Valerie. Listen, I just had a request for a paper shredder. What's interesting is that they don't want the shredder just for the purpose of shredding confidential material. They also plan to use the shredded paper as packing material to replace those Styrofoam peanuts. Isn't that a great idea? What do you think about doing the same thing at Corporate?"

"I don't really know. Linda does most of the packing and shipping in the office."

"Valerie, why don't you ask Linda what she thinks? Please tell her I will talk to her when I get back."

A few days pass. "Hi, Linda."

"Good morning, David. Welcome back. How was your trip?"

"It was fine, thanks. Did Valerie have a chance to talk to you about using shredded paper as stuffing in packages we ship?"

"Yes, she did."

"Do you think we should try it?"

"David, I've been doing that for the last two years."

"You're kidding!"

"No. It works quite well. Sometimes I put newspaper in the bottom, with the object I'm mailing in the box surrounded by shredded paper. Other times, I mix the Styrofoam peanuts with the shredded paper. Many times I spread the shredded paper on top of the object I'm mailing."

"Have you ever had any problems with broken or damaged goods?"

"No, and I haven't had any complaints in the last two years."

"We don't buy those styrofoam peanuts, do we?"

"No. I just save whatever I get in the mail and re-use it. The shredded paper has never been in short supply. We always have plenty of that." We laugh.

"Linda, please share this with the other divisions, so they'll start to use their shredded paper. I also want you to call Dick Base at Everlasting Valve Corporation, New Jersey, and tell him you've been using shredded paper for packing over the last two years. This information will reassure him to give it a try." 🔥

> *Shredded, confidential reports won't reveal your company's secrets—there are easier methods of betrayal.*

THE MORAL OF THIS STORY

1.

2.

3.

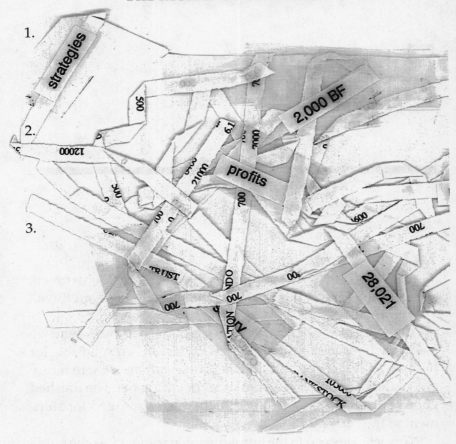

71
Cigarette Butts

"**W**ell, that finishes the tour for the machining department. We'll now proceed to the assembly department in plant three."

A few minutes pass.

"You will notice we have several assembly benches where we assemble traps and other products. Each man is responsible for his own quality inspection and, of course, has the right to refuse any materials he receives from other departments. The finished goods are sent to the paint booth and then packaged for shipment to the customer."

"Now let's proceed to the humidifier department." As the guide leads the tour of customers, partners, and representatives to the next department, a customer in the back of the group casually takes the cigarette out of his mouth and throws it on the shop floor near Gard Dolph.

"Excuse me, sir," replies Gard. "Would you please pick up your cigarette butt?"

The gentleman stops in his tracks, looks at Gard and bends over to pick up his cigarette.

"There's a place over there where you can throw it away. Thank you for helping to keep our plant clean. We're very proud of it!"

Later that day, Gary Ford, who was leading the tour, tells a story about another gentleman in the tour who overheard what happened and carried his cigarette in his hand during the entire tour. 🔥

> *The customer is not always right. They cannot break our core values—that includes littering.*

The Moral Of This Story

1. Don't litter—that means in the office, shop and even the parking lot! It's a dirty habit and we DO take a lot of pride in how clean our facilities and grounds are.

2. Being the bearer of bad news is always difficult—especially when it's a small thing. When Gard asked the man to pick up his cigarette butt, he was the bearer of bad news and it definitely was a little thing—especially to the man who threw his cigarette butt on the floor. I have given bad news to people before on major issues, but I find it difficult to do so on small things. I have seen people throw cigarette butts on the floor and never asked them to pick them up—even after I heard this story. I wish I had the courage of Gard. Maybe after writing this story I will.

3. Don't get personal. When giving constructive criticism, no matter what the topic, do not get personal. Keep it strictly professional, critiquing the subject at hand and not the person.

4. Learning is a two-way street. I hope the readers of my stories learn from them. I do when I write them. You can learn something from anybody, if you want to. Thanks, Gard, for the lesson!

72
Finger Painting

"**H**i! My name is David Armstrong."

"Hello, my name is Rich Peters."

"So, tell me, Rich, what do you do at Everlasting Valve Corporation here in New Jersey?"

"I paint."

"What do you paint — the building, portraits, billboards, houses?" I smile.

Rich laughs and says, "No, I paint the valves after they have been assembled." Rich leads me to the paint booth.

"So, Rich. Show me how you paint these valves."

"Well, when we have large valves such as this one, I paint them with a spray gun. But when I have small valves, I dip them into a can of paint. It's quicker and we get a nice, smooth finish."

"Rich, I see that you held on to the handle as you dipped the valve into the paint. What about the handle? How do you paint it?"

"I was told to use a paint brush." Rich pulls out a paint brush and paints the remaining part of the handle.

"But, Rich, the paint doesn't match. One portion has a smooth surface; the other part has brush strokes."

"I know, that's why I've made a change to the process. Now I put on plastic gloves to keep my hands clean and dip the whole valve and handle into the paint. I pull it out and put it on these hooks. When I'm done, I take off the gloves. Not only are we getting a better paint job, but I'm able to paint more valves in less time."

THE MORAL OF THIS STORY

1. Maybe even a thumb! Many solutions to our problems lie in the right side of our brain. We must be creative. We cannot just follow the way it's always been done (i.e. Rich started using gloves instead of a paint brush to finish the handle). Some have referred to this as tunnel vision. Open up your mind when solving a problem and look outside the walls of the tunnel to solve that problem.

2. Being creative takes practice — try this for fun.

```
•   •   •

•   •   •

•   •   •
```

The object is to connect all nine dots by drawing no more than four straight lines, and without lifting the pencil from the paper. Try this exercise *before* reading the solutions on the next page.

3. How can you see through a tunnel? What if the tunnel was made of glass and you were in the ocean? You could see all the fish and coral. What if the tunnel was in the sky and it took you to a floating city? What if the tunnel went through fire? My point is, why must a tunnel be underground or made of cement? Open your mind.

4. Maybe we should hire science fiction writers. Every company needs one, maybe more, if we want to solve our problems in new and creative ways.

Answer to No. 2 from the story, *Finger Painting:*

The key to the puzzle lies in your ability to redefine the context in which you see the nine dots. The most common answer is the first solution shown below. Go *outside* the box of dots.

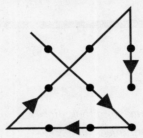

Some additional solutions are as follows:

• If the paper is folded along a line equidistant between the first two rows of dots, and also folded along another line equidistant between the second and third rows of dots, then the dots will touch each other in three triplets and connect along a single line.

• Use a very big brush to cover all the dots with one broad stroke.

• A fourth solution comes from non-Euclidian geometry, in which parallel lines meet at infinity; therefore extend a line through one row to infinity, then zigzag back through the middle row, and back again through the last row.

• A fifth is that when you hold the page so that only its edge shows, all the dots are on that one same line.

Exercise taken from *Future Perfect*, by Stanley M. Davis, Addison-Wesley Publishing Company, Inc. *"I would highly recommend you read this book for thinking into the future."*

73
My Name Is...

Dedicated to: Dick Carter, who took pictures
for our employees' book.

Long, long ago, Adam Armstrong would spend part of his day walking through the office and shop, talking to the people. Adam always addressed everyone by their first name and asked how their family was doing. He knew the names of the children, the wife — heck, he even knew the name of the dog! Many times Adam would ask how well an employee's son had played the night before in a ball game. You see, Adam not only knew all the names of the people and their pets, but he knew when special events were taking place in their lives, such as important ball games.

Lawrence Armstrong, Adam's son, also spent a great deal of time talking to the people. Lawrence, often referred to as Army, knew the names of the wives and children as well. Maybe he didn't know the pet's name, but he kept close to the people and knew of special events in their lives.

Gus Armstrong, son of Lawrence Armstrong, spent time with the people. Gus didn't know the dog's name, and seldom knew of a special event. He did know most of the people's names. Now,

I find myself carrying on the role of talking to the people. I don't know many of the wives' names, nor the children—heck, I don't even know if they have a dog. With all of the new people hired, it's becoming very difficult for me to remember everyone's name. Being 1,500 miles away from a plant doesn't help matters, either. It bothers me! It bothers me that I don't know everybody's name. It should bother you, too. 🔥

> *Share your first name with someone and make a friend.*

THE MORAL OF THIS STORY

1. Name tags are not the answer. You must hang out together, have lunch together, tell jokes to each other, share experiences, tell stories, and become friends. Friends use first names and *don't forget* them. Friends normally work well together. Strangers don't work as well together. If you know everybody's first name, it will mean that you are comfortable and familiar with each other. Learn everyone's first name.

2. What's the name of that person? Many times I have asked this question while talking with someone. Too many times I've heard the answer, "I don't know." "Why don't you know?" I ask. "They work across the parking lot and I never see them"... or, "They work in another department, not my department"... or, "They work in the shop and I work in the office." Sometimes I hear, "Oh, they're Manpower." None of these excuses are good— become familiar and use the first name of people you work with. Hint—you work with *everybody* at Armstrong.

3. It's more difficult to lay someone off when you know their first name. If you don't begin using first names, you will become just a number. Many companies no longer know the employees' names and refer to them by a number. That should bother you! If you're just a number, it's easy for the company and its leaders not to be personally connected with you, to be familiar with you, to care about you, and this leads to layoffs.

4. The *first* way to prove to someone that you care is to know their name.

5. **Televisions throughout Armstrong... give five minutes of video time** and introduce newly hired, retiring, and long tenure employees. Watching television may help us learn names. It's sad to think we know actors' names better than people we work with every day.

6. **Armstrong's Employee Directory has photographs.** Dick Carter took pictures of our employees. We added their names and the department they work in below the picture. This Employee Directory is left at break areas, lunch rooms, etc. for people to look through to learn first names.

Stories
to
inspire
self-management

74
From Rags To Riches

O nce a week, we collect dirty shop rags and send them out to be cleaned. Through the years, the rags had become a valuable commodity since the employees used them to clean their machines and their hands. These rags had become s-o-o-o-o valuable that they were kept—under lock and key!

Foreman: "I want you to gather up the dirty shop rags in our department. Make sure you count them. Take them next door so they can be sent out to be cleaned. They'll give you clean rags. Make sure they give you the same amount you turn in."

New employee: "Who's got them and where can I find them (as he held a rag in his hand)?"

"Go to each person in our department and ask for their rags."

"How many will I get?"

"Somewhere between 50 and 75."

So the employee goes around collecting the rags, making sure to count them and walks to Plant I to turn them in. When he arrives, he approaches someone working in the office. "Excuse me, I have the dirty shop rags from our department. Who do I turn them into for clean rags?"

Shop rag keeper: "I'll be happy to take them. How many do you have?"

"Sixty-five."

"Throw them in that red barrel where we keep the dirty rags. I'll unlock the cabinet and get your clean rags."

"Do you have to keep them locked up?"

"You bet. These things are priceless. Everybody needs more than what they're willing to turn in. There was a man named Jack who died recently. We found 400 shop rags locked in his tool chest." 🔥

So little done, so much to do.

THE MORAL OF THIS STORY

1. Practice self-management — no matter how small the responsibility. We practice self-management a hundred different ways, but we missed this one. We will no longer count our rags when returning them. Rags will not be kept under lock and key. We trust our people. Self-management is not only for the big items, such as time clocks, open cash registers in the cafeteria and quality control; but also for little things, such as rags. You confuse people when you practice self-management for the big items, but not for the little items. Anybody, at any time, will be allowed to get as many rags as they need.

2. Practice self-management and receive value added. Locking up the rags and spending time to find somebody with a key is time-consuming and has no value added. After all, the price of new rags is not that expensive. We always seem to be understaffed; maybe this is one reason why. If we don't support self-management with little things, how many other exceptions will there be for not practicing self management? Where do you draw the line?

3. A familiar sight provokes no attention. This was a wise Chinese proverb. We are very alert and proud of our self-management at Armstrong; yet, shop rags, a common sight, had a different set of rules that did not include self-management. How many more "familiar sights" are there in our shop and office where we have not applied the rules of self-management. Seek, find and change these to what we know works — self-management.

To be continued...

75
From Rags To Riches II

There I was, doing what I do best... telling a story. As I told the story "From Rags to Riches" to Doug Criswell, 1st shift foreman, and Lester Newbre, 2nd shift foreman, a smile came to their faces. Based on their smiles, I knew I had a classic.

After finishing the morals, Lester asks, "What about the gloves?"

David: "Do we lock those up, too?"

Lester: "Sure, they're locked up in that filing cabinet." Lester points to a cabinet in a corner.

David: "It seems to me the rules that apply to rags also should apply to gloves. We shouldn't lock them up. What do you think, Doug?"

Doug: Doug nods in agreement and says, "It's okay with me. But we need to let our people know they can pick them up whenever they wish, or what good is it to unlock the cabinet to the rags and gloves?"

David: "You're right, Doug. That's why I'm telling you this story. I want you to share this story about the rags. And now you can add gloves to the story!"

Lester: "David, did you know they lock up the food in our lunch room?"

David: "No, it's out in the open with all the money."
(See 'The Cafeteria,' a story in *Managing by Storying Around*.

Lester: "Yes, that's right, but the extra supplies are locked up."

David: "You're kidding!"

Doug nods in agreement.

David: "I don't understand why we lock up the *extra* food, when food and money is kept out in the open? I'll look into that, but please share our story about the rags and gloves."

When I reach the lunch room I find Richard Wright and Charlie Kauffman restocking the shelves with food that had been purchased at break. Charlie and Rich are responsible for restocking the shelves. Sure enough, I notice the locks on the cupboards.

David: "Charlie! Rich! Can you clarify something for me? But first I want to tell you a story, and the title is 'From Rags to Riches'."

As I finish the story, they agree we should not keep our rags or gloves under lock and key. Then I ask, "Do you know why we keep the food locked up, and yet leave money out in the open?"

Charlie: "No, but if you think we should take the locks off, we'll do it right now."

David: "It doesn't matter what I think; I want to know what you guys think."

Rich: "I think we can take the locks off. I don't have a problem with it."

Charlie: "I don't have a problem with it either. It probably makes good sense."

David: "Charlie, we're going to have to make sure we let everybody know the locks are off the cupboard."

As we talk, I hear **BANG, BANG.** I turn and see Rich is already removing one of the locks by smacking it with a screwdriver; knocking it free.

David: "Rich, now that's what I call urgency! Charlie, will you help me spread the word?"

Charlie: "Consider it done!"

David: "You know, Charlie, I'll bet this would make a great story!"

So little done; so much to do.

THE MORAL OF THIS STORY

1. Practice self-management—no matter how small the responsibility. We practice self-management in a hundred different ways, but we missed this one. We should not lock up our gloves and extra food. We trust our people with money and food in the open, so why not trust them with the gloves and extra food? Our gloves and food supplies are no longer under lock and key. Self-management is not only for big items; such as time clocks, money on the table in the cafeteria and quality control; but also for little things, such as gloves and food. Practicing self-management for the big items does not smell of integrity when you won't do the same for little items. Anybody, at anytime, should be allowed to get gloves or find food in the cupboards.

2. Practice self-management and receive value added. Locking up the gloves and spending time to find somebody with a key is time consuming and has no value added. After all, the price of new gloves is not that expensive. We always seem to be understaffed; maybe this is one reason. If we don't support self-management with little things, how many other exceptions will there be for not practicing self-management? Where do you draw the line?

3. A familiar sight provokes no attention. We are very alert and proud of our self-management at Armstrong; yet, gloves and extra food items, a common sight, had a different set of rules which did not include self-management. How many more "familiar" sights are there in our shop or office where we have not used the rules of self-management? Seek, find and change to what we know works—self-management.

4. Different stories can have the same morals. You will notice the "From Rags to Riches" stories, part I and part II, are different stories. Yet, each has the same morals and the same quote. There is no doubt one story will affect one person more than another. Why? If the person is familiar with the story, it becomes more personal. This happens when someone has lived the story they are reading or hearing. This makes the morals and quotes more believable. For example, some people have lived the "Rags" story and therefore the morals mean something. Others who have *not* lived the "Rags" story, but have problems getting gloves so they relate to the morals in the "Gloves" story. If there was only one story about the "Rags," those having problems with the gloves may not believe the morals.

76
How Much?

The following story is dedicated to Forrest Butterfield for telling the story (we need more storytellers) and to Jan Butterfield who made this story possible.

Forrest Butterfield, manufacturing engineer, has been working for Armstrong International, Inc., Michigan for many years. Therefore, his wife, Jan, is covered under our health insurance plan. Recently, Jan injured her knee and she decided to see her doctor. When she got to his office, the doctor asked, "So, Jan, why have you come to see me today?"

"It's my knee, doctor. I hurt it a few days ago and it's really bothering me."

"Let's see what's wrong." The doctor slowly moves Jan's leg up and down, watching the movement in her knee. "Jan, I think we need to have an MRI Scan done. It's not cheap; it's $1,000."

Jan gasps, **"How much?"**

The doctor answers, "Yes, I know it's expensive, but..."

Jan interrupts, "Will this tell you what's wrong with my knee?"

"Yes, I believe it will."

"One thousand dollars; that's a lot of money. I'm going to have to think about it. Maybe my knee will get better. I'll let you know after I talk to my husband."

"I understand, Jan. But we really should look at it soon before it gets worse."

Several days pass and Jan's knee isn't improving. One of her neighbors sees her and mentions, "Jan, there's a sign-up sheet at Bronson Hospital. Dr. Burnett is conducting a survey and needs 10 volunteers to have a free MRI for undiagnosed knee problems. It may not be too late if you sign up today."

Jan asks (as she grabs a pencil), "What was the doctor's name?
"Dr. Burnett."

"Thanks!" Jan immediately went to Bronson to sign up. She was one of the first 10 and she received the MRI at no cost to the Armstrong insurance plan.

Some people feel self-management can't work.

THE MORAL OF THIS STORY

1. You practice self-management at home — why not at work? You balance your checkbook; allocate capital for furniture, cars and appliances; perform home repairs; schedule your time and even create a house budget. For those people who do not believe in self-management, they should ask themselves, "If people *can* self-manage at home, why not at work?"

2. Why does self-management work? It's *simple* to practice. It must be; we practice it at home every day. There is also an element of *ownership* in self-management that makes people use common sense, feel accountable for their decisions and care about what they do. Everybody likes to *play the game* and become involved. That builds *pride* and a desire to do the best one can do. If we encourage self-management more people will be involved with their ideas; and the more ideas, the better our chances of success!

3. Nothing is free — not even Jan's MRI. Jan had to work hard to get that free MRI scan. It took one extra trip to sign up, time to fill out several survey forms and waiting in line with nine other people for the Scan. Self-management often requires extra work, but remember that you impose that work on yourself because you care.

77
The Pilot's Job Description

It was a quiet Monday morning in Stuart, Florida. Everyone was working in the office on projects; secretaries were wrapping up those loose ends from the week before and preparing for the new week at hand.

I walked to the other side of the building for a cup of hot chocolate. The company pilots were in the office talking to the receptionist. When they saw me, both Tom Boone and Steve LaFalce said, "Hi Dave!"

I said, "Hello, how long are you going to be in town?"

Tom said, "Until Thursday morning when we fly back to Michigan."

"What are you going to do to keep busy for the next few days?"

Tom and Steve responded, "We have to clean the plane, make sure it's refueled, prepare the flight plan and do our safety check."

"That sounds good," and I proceeded to make my cup of hot chocolate.

Steve LaFalce approached me in private. "David, I've noticed you've been writing many stories on Armstrong and its people. I would like to offer my services in helping proofread the stories. You're probably not aware, but I hold a graduate degree in English. I would be more than happy to check for punctuation, spelling and grammar errors."

I immediately accepted his offer and took him to my secretary. She gave him a book with approximately 40 stories to be proofread during the week. When I received the book full of corrections, without the content being changed, I realized we had to use Steve's services. From that day forward, all stories have gone to Steve for proofreading.

> *Believe in the spirit of self-management.*
> *It's greater than any policy, order or job description.*

THE MORAL OF THIS STORY

1. Were you looking for a job description in this story? Do you remember the story about job descriptions in my first book titled, "Managing By Storying Around?" We have none. Why? Because this promotes everyone helping one another and not just performing their written job description.

2. Sometimes people volunteer before being asked. Steve knew he could help since he had a master's degree in English. This story supports our belief that job descriptions are not required.

3. Self-management is something you live each day. Maybe this is the best tool we have toward achieving success. If it is, how can we encourage it throughout the company?

78
The President's Son is Late for Work

It is 1977 and the president's son, David Armstrong, is driving to work one morning. As David approaches the factory, he knows he's going to be late.

As I get out of the car, I think to myself, "Oh boy, I'm late. I wonder if I can sneak in. I'm only a few minutes late—maybe no one will notice me."

So, I pick a side door and quickly try to slip in. When I take a few steps, I hear that familiar sound… **Bam, Bam, Bam.** As it echoes through the factory from all four corners, the noise gets louder and louder… **Bam, Bam, Bam.** I thought, "I know what that sound is. It's the sound of hammers hitting the benches by all of my friends in the factory. This is the tradition at Armstrong International, Inc., Michigan when someone comes in late—they hammer you in."

Well, let me tell you, I was embarrassed! I immediately put my head down and went to my bench. Later that day, everybody was joking and teasing me and asking how it felt. I don't think I was late the rest of that summer, but I did have the opportunity to hammer in others who were late.

The year is now 1991 and I am visiting the Milton, Florida, plant. They have just finished watching a videotape about Armstrong where they saw the people in the factory hammering someone in as a demonstration of how to help support self-management.

As I talked to several guys in the plant at Milton, they told me, "David, we just saw the video. We want you to know we started hammering people in when they were late. It really gets their attention!"

As I approached the next guy, I asked, "What do you think about hammering in people who are late?"

"Let me tell you, David, they hammered me in not once, but twice. I didn't like it. It's embarrassing. It makes you not want to come in late again."

"I know that feeling. It happened to me."

"You mean they actually hammered you in?"

"Everybody gets hammered in," I replied. "There are no exceptions."

> *Self-management needs a little help now and then.*

THE MORAL OF THIS STORY

1. Self-management needs support from coworkers. There are occasions when coworkers must help enforce self-management—like when they hammered me in. Why wait for a leader to solve a problem of absenteeism; go ahead and hammer someone in.

2. You can hide from your boss, but not from your coworkers.

3. Sometimes self-management needs support from management. There are people who will not manage themselves, nor can coworkers; therefore, management must enforce the rules.

4. Anyone can be hammered in. If David Armstrong can be hammered in, anyone can. There are no exceptions! This is one of our core values; fairness.

5. Who will be the first to swing their hammer? If everybody waits for somebody else to start, it will never happen. When they hammered me in, somebody had the guts to start it. "Thank you" for helping me become a better person.

6. Why does a hammer struck on a bench prevent people from coming to work late? It's embarrassing, uncomfortable and not worth the extra few minutes—take it from David Armstrong, who learned the hard way!

Stories about tradition

CHAPTER XVII

79
A Family Tradition Of Fishing And Hunting

During one of my visits to Armstrong International, Inc. in Michigan, I asked, "Where is everybody?"

The general manager responded, "What do you mean?"

"I've spent the last four hours walking through the shop and it looks like only half the people are here."

"David, did you forget fishing season opened this week?"

"Oh, that's right, I forgot! So that's where all the people went!"

Several months pass.

Once again, I find myself asking, "Where are all the people? I know it's not fishing season."

The general manager said, "David, obviously you're not a hunter either because deer season opened and the plant will be half empty for the next two weeks."

"You're right. I always forget when deer season opens."

Another month passes.

A secretary asked, "David, are you going to come to the Christmas party?"

"I don't know. When is it?"

She answered, "It will be on Tuesday the 24th since Christmas falls on Wednesday. We break at lunch and go to the recreation building. We will have a quick announcement by top management, some goodies to eat, and then we go home."

"I would really like to share this special tradition with everyone, but it's too close to Christmas. I could get stranded in Michigan, due to bad weather, while my family is in Florida celebrating Christmas. I think I'd better stay home." 🔥

> **Don't lose your traditions; you could lose your people.**

THE MORAL OF THIS STORY

1. Some waste is needed. Be careful when you make changes for the sake of efficiency or value added. If you remove your traditions which seem wasteful on the surface, you may cause other problems.

2. Traditions such as Christmas parties and hunting and fishing create this family environment. Even with all the changes taking place, some things need to remain the same. Traditions can offer that stability, feeling of comfort, something you can count on year in and year out. The future only offers more change at a faster pace; *traditions offer comfort.*

3. You have more traditions in your company than you realize. If you need proof, start counting them on a sheet of paper. At Armstrong we have several (i.e., a steak fry, the company picnic, fishing season, deer season, free turkeys at Thanksgiving, hams at Easter, lunch during Christmas and our Halloween party). Now ask yourself, "Why do we have so many?—Because they're needed."

80
Stories Becoming Tradition

It is early morning and you're arriving at Armstrong International, Inc., Michigan for a scheduled meeting. You park in visitors parking and walk to the reception area. As you pass through the double doors, you are impressed with the appearance of the reception area. You give your name to the receptionist.

While waiting, you glance around the room and notice a storybook.

You begin to read the first few stories when you're interrupted, "Your meeting will begin now. Would you please follow me to our conference room?"

You walk down a long hallway, past a swinging door, and proceed down the steps to the conference room. As you're walking toward the conference room, you see people gathered around a large table. You approach the table and take your seat.

During the meeting, your eyes begin to wander and all of a sudden you notice beautifully framed pictures hanging on the wall. There is a set of 12. "Oh, wait! These aren't pictures, what are they?" When you take a coffee break, you get up to inspect one closely. It's another story about Armstrong which has been put into a picture frame.

Following the meeting, you go on a shop tour. You notice how clean the building looks and how motivated all the workers are. As you're talking to one of the machinists, you notice another picture frame. You know what's in it, but you take a closer look to make sure. "Sure enough, it's another story!" This time the story is about the person operating the machine.

The tour continues and you stop to get a drink. That cool, refreshing water brings you back to life and as you look up, you see yet another story. Oh, wait, not one... but 15, thumb-tacked to the bulletin board.

You begin to realize storytelling must be a way of life at Armstrong. Everywhere you look you see stories!

Throughout the day you continue to see stories, and a few of these stories you've recognized as being applied by the people you've seen. 🔥

> *We must tell stories; we're their leaders.*

THE MORAL OF THIS STORY

1. Storytelling has always been a tradition within families... now make it a tradition at Armstrong. For storytelling to become a tradition, you must make stories visible in as many locations as possible. They must become familiar sights. They must be heard often. There must be no doubt in everyone's mind that storytelling is a tradition at Armstrong.

2. Why should storytelling become a tradition—or anything else for that matter? People believe in tradition; they follow tradition. If you can make your idea a tradition, giving it the status of a tradition, you'll have a better chance of succeeding.

3. Traditions live forever. Items of importance should not be here today, gone tomorrow. They should live forever. If you make them traditions, they will!

81
The Ball And Chain

This story begins with a group of manufacturing engineers huddled in the corner of a manufacturing engineering department. Their discussion is one of some importance. Their friend and co-worker, Pat Armstrong, is getting married and they don't know what to get him.

Pat's older and wiser brother, (that's me), interrupts the group. "Excuse me guys, I think I know what we can give Pat for his wedding. Since the tradition of this company is to give the ball and chain to everybody who is getting married, why don't we give that to Patrick?"

Andy Schirk: "That's a great idea! Who's got the ball and chain?"

Mickey Gaines: "I think Grant Kain knows."

Jim Arjmand: "Let's get the ball and chain and find Pat."

For those of you who don't know what the ball and chain is, let me give you the following definition: On one end of the chain is a shackle with a padlock. This is fastened around the leg of the employee about to be married. On the other end is a weighted ball—10 pounds for men and five pounds for women. *All* employees who are getting married must wear this ball and chain for one full day at work. They are presented with a photograph capturing the special moment of tradition.

I said, "Patrick is in a meeting at Corporate. Let's go interrupt the meeting and put the ball and chain on him. Does anybody want to join me?"

Everybody smiles and marches with me out the door. We approach the office of Ron Schlesch, vice president of Manufacturing and Engineering, and I say with a serious voice, "Excuse me, Ron. Could we have 60 seconds of Patrick's time? There's a group of friends that need to see him."

Seven or eight guys crowd past me and into the office to put the ball and chain on Patrick's leg. Patrick knows there's no escape so he sits back and lets everybody have their fun. 🔥

> *You grow up the day you have your first real laugh—*
> *at yourself.*
> — *Ethel Barrymore, actress*

THE MORAL OF THIS STORY

1. Traditions are what give a company its character... and character is what attracts and keeps people.

2. Only traditions such as the ball and chain reveal true working relationships. We have Armstrong associates, characters, crew members, team players and family members. We are trying to cultivate a team atmosphere with these words. But, these are only words. The best way to determine if people honestly get along is seeing them playing together in a friendly fashion, not by using fancy titles.

3. Be careful when changing your traditions. A tradition may seem like a small thing, but it's important to your employees. They take it seriously—that's all that matters.

4. When recruiting, talk about your traditions. This makes your company more personal, friendly and alive; not so cold, uncaring, and impersonal.

5. Fun people are productive people. They tend to spur their coworkers toward higher production levels, particularly if they are serving in a leadership capacity.

PAT

CLAY

82
The Nail That Stands Out Gets Hammered Down

It is in the early years of Armstrong-Yoshitake when this story is told.

Frank Bowser was the sales manager, with Tom Grubka and Tom Rockwell as product specialists. Frank was chosen as sales manager due to his knowledge of the product line and the market. An added benefit was his understanding of the Japanese language and culture. During Frank's visits to Japan he had identified two companies which were best suited for selling Armstrong products. He cited Yoshitake-Works, Ltd. as one of those companies. During his visits, he studied the Japanese language and their customs; that was our first step toward success.

As we were talking one day, I said, "Frank, I understand we have three visitors coming from Yoshitake-Works, Ltd. I wonder why the Japanese always travel in groups?"

"In Japan they have the saying, "The nail that stands out gets hammered down, answered Frank."

"What does it mean?"

"In the Japanese business culture, everybody works as a team. The boss sits with the workers—not in a separate office. This is also why you don't see them travel by themselves. In each of these cases, they would be singled out as being special and it's against their culture in Japan."

Frank continued, "Here's something else you should know, David. In Japan, they put great importance on doing business with friends. You become friends before doing business."

"Why?"

"That's their culture, they feel comfortable and trust friends. So go on their tours, and maybe even spend some vacation time with them. After you do this, you can talk business."

"Thanks, Frank! Since everything is so different in Japan, I really don't know how to act. I'm going to find as much material as possible to help me learn about Japanese culture." 🔥

> *While in Rome, do as the Romans do.*

THE MORAL OF THIS STORY

1. Presidents meet with presidents; vice presidents meet with vice presidents. Protocol in Japan is very important! It's not proper for the president of a Japanese company to meet with someone of lower rank. This shows a lack of respect.

2. There is a ritual exchange of business cards. In America, we hand out business cards like a deck of cards (throwing them on the table). In Japan, however, a business card must be clean and unsoiled, with no folding marks on the card. You must present the card with the printed side up facing the receiver, so they can read it easily. You should also hold your card not in your palm, but with both hands on the edges. When you receive their business card, use both hands; and, most importantly, study the card a few moments before putting it away. This shows respect for the person's title. *Never* write on the card in front of the Japanese. Is your business card in English with the language of the country you're visiting on the other side?

3. Seat the highest-ranked visitor in the center position furthest from the door, with the highest-ranked host sitting opposite. Seat other persons opposite from their counterparts. The lowest-ranked person sits near the door.

4. Refreshments should be served immediately upon seating.
Use good tea sets, not styrofoam cups. Drink together in silence;
this is a ritual which promotes harmony and trust. *Do not* discuss
business until finished drinking.

5. Finally, be careful with the word "Yes." The Japanese
acknowledge your statement with "Yes," even if they do not
intend to agree. They are only saying "Yes," that they understand
you.

83
Our Company Picnic

Dedicated to: Janet Babcock, Mike Furey, Etta Griffin,
*   Howard King, Karen Lippens, Tim McCollum,*
*   Brad Neumueller, Diane Reece, Mike Talbot,*
*   Linda Tokarski, Dan Torrans*

The loud roar of an engine, a black puff of smoke, and a strong odor of diesel fuel filled the air as the busses left. The busses were heading home to Armstrong International, Inc., Michigan with their seats filled with Armstrong employees and their families. Some people followed in their cars. The company picnic, which had been held on company grounds for so many years, had been held this day at Michigan Adventure Amusement Park. The picnic was a success and it all began one day when...

Armstag had just finished planning the same old company picnic. Board members had decided to volunteer for the same old positions as before to make the picnic.

Suddenly, Dan Torrans said, "Too bad we couldn't do what my sister's company did and go to Michigan Adventure Amusement Park."

The air was still, then suddenly the question was answered, "Why not? The worst the company can do is say no."

Immediately the room was filled with excitement. What used to be "who can *we* get to do that?" became "what can I do to help?" Questions and answers were coming from all the members.

"What about the retirees? They won't go."

"Let's offer them a bingo night in January."

"Hey, they have grandchildren, I bet they would love to see them have fun at the amusement park."

"What about the drive up there?"

"Let's charter some busses to take people up there."

"Busses cost too much."

"How do we know that unless we check it out."

"With Armstrong and Armstag paying for my ticket to the amusement park, I wouldn't mind paying for the bus ride."

> *Add life to your traditions, change them.*

THE MORAL OF THIS STORY

1. Traditions can become outdated... even boring, unnoticed if they never change. Thanks to Armstag, our family picnic was very successful because it was more fun for the children at the amusement park. It was also different, which brought life back to this old tradition.

2. People change, and so must traditions. Traditions must be modified so they better fit today's needs. Today people are always in a hurry. At the old picnic, they would have come, eaten their lunch, and quickly left. Taking a bus ride and visiting an amusement park for the *whole* day gives plenty of opportunity for people to experience friendship and time together.

3. Don't lose the meaning of our traditions. When changing our traditions, don't forget why they were started. Our family picnic was a form of celebration and having fun. But equally important was the opportunity for the families to get together and become better friends. Putting them on a bus, as Armstag had recommended, allowed everybody to talk during the long bus ride.

4. Traditions changed to make them better... is good because it helps keep them alive. Changing a tradition to save money or time to increase production is wrong.

84
God Bless America ♪

I t was early morning and the Coliseum was filled. The lights were dimmed and you could just make out the faces of the people. Four people walked onto the stage which had been located close to the center of the Coliseum's floor. The loudspeakers above rang out with the words,

"Would you please bow your heads for this morning's prayer."

At the end of the prayer, a bright spotlight shined on the American flag which hung above the stage. Again, the words rang out,

"Would you please stand and face the flag to say the 'Pledge of Allegiance'."

Everybody stood up, took their right hand, and covered their heart, and the words were said.

"I pledge Allegiance to the Flag of the United States of America and to the Republic for which it stands, one nation, under God, indivisible, with liberty and justice for all."

I was a guest that day, and I thank Dianne Secen and Phil Bommarito for inviting me to Internet's Weekend of the Diamonds. Dianne and Phil are Amway distributors and wanted me to experience Dexter Yager's organization called Internet. What I witnessed was person after person getting on stage and talking about dreams, freedom, and how to be winners. Each of these speakers loved to tell stories—stories about family, love, religion, and business. Later that evening I had a chance to meet Dexter, and for over two hours, one storyteller to another, we swapped stories and philosophies of business. 🔥

> *I have dreams that take my breath away.*
> — Dexter Yager, Amway Corp.

THE MORAL OF THIS STORY

1. I pledge allegiance to the flag… It felt good, saying the "Pledge of Allegiance." Ask yourself if you remembered all of the words? Be honest! Just as a story must be retold to stay alive, so must we repeat the "Pledge of Allegiance" so our children and our children's children don't forget it, so we don't forget it. We should fly the American flag proudly. We just purchased several flags, eight feet in height, with gold tassels, hanging on a wooden pole, held in place with a shiny brass base. The final touch is an eagle perched at the top of the pole. What a beautiful sight. We shared that sight—we put flags everywhere. You should hear the positive comments.

2. Our Father, who art in heaven… Religion has been taken out of the schools, and that's a shame. Businesses have also forgotten their religious roots, and that's a shame. Leaders who believe in the Bible normally practice the Golden Rule—Do Unto Others As You Would Have Them Do Unto You. That makes your place of work more enjoyable.

3. Let the dreamers come to me. I like dreamers, for they are the ones who make America great and improve mankind's existence. The Pilgrims dreamt of a land where they could worship freely, George Eastman (Kodak) dreamt of capturing memories on film, Henry Ford dreamt of making cars affordable for the common man, and Martin Luther King had a dream, as do all great leaders. We need more dreamers in our world, and Dexter Yager is right when he says: "Don't let anybody steal your dream."

4. Catch the spirit! When the day started with a prayer, followed by the "Pledge of Allegiance," you could feel it! You could feel the spirit of the people, and that spirit grew as the day grew. Sometimes we take our country for granted. Be proud of our country, catch the spirit that our forefathers had, and this country will continue to prosper.

Stories about legends, myths and tall tales

CHAPTER XVIII

85
A Job For Life?

He sat nervously in his chair, looking straight ahead, while anticipating the next question. The next question came as quickly as the first. He thought to himself, "Am I answering the questions correctly? Will they hire me?"

As the interview came to a close, the interviewer asked, "Do you have any questions I can answer about Armstrong International, Inc.?"

"Yes. I was told, during my other interviews, if you're hired by Armstrong, you're hired for life. Is this true?"

"No. That's not true. What should have been said is that most of the people who come to work at Armstrong seldom quit. Our turnover rate is very low. I think that's because we have good working conditions, care about each other, have a good health care program, and we pay very well."

"I was also told people don't get fired at Armstrong."

"No, that's not true either. We have fired people. But it's also true that one of the best ways to have a long and fruitful career at Armstrong is to do a good job and get along with the people at Armstrong. Remember, we are a tight group, very much like a family. The quickest way to get into trouble at Armstrong is by *not* getting along with each other."

A company is known by the people it employs.

THE MORAL OF THIS STORY

1. Many companies *don't* hire their employees' family members. We have found that hiring an employee's sister, brother, father, spouse, etc., to be a benefit. We only hire those family members, however, if they are qualified and *only* if we have a job to offer.

2. A job for life cannot be promised. But take comfort in our history of how we treat employees. Does Armstrong have a good or bad reputation in regards to employment? Take comfort in your answer or leave Armstrong if you're concerned.

3. To build a great company requires great people! To *attract* great people, our company must have a good reputation in dealing with people. Few layoffs and terminations are a must! We must be very careful who we hire or we jeopardize this. To *keep* great people we must have low employee turnover.

86
A Sacred Cow!

On April 6, 1992, a Monday morning in the accounting department, someone said, "We just received our Accounts Receivable Report and several of our representatives (reps) are overdue. Should we call them or send a letter?"

"No, let's wait. They're one of our largest reps. Let's give them another month."

On May 4, 1992, "We just received this month's Accounts Receivable Report. Those same reps are now 60 days late. Should we call them now?"

"Why don't you give them a nice, friendly call and ask if there's a problem? And, if so, can we help?"

A few hours pass. "I called the reps. They said they would get checks to us this week and bring their accounts up-to-date. They're having trouble collecting from their customers and money is a little tight right now."

On June 1, 1992, several reps were 90 to 120 days late. "Didn't we get those checks that were promised?"

"Only one check came in."

"I think it's time to visit the sales department and talk about stopping shipments."

A meeting is called with accounting and sales. "We have a problem with several reps who are past due and not paying their bills. Should we stop their shipments until they become current?"

"Ahhhh, I don't know! You know how Gus Armstrong feels about the reps. If we cut them off, they'll probably call Gus. Gus will call us and want to know why we're giving bad service to the reps. He will tell us to trust our reps."

"Yes, I know. But they're past due and showing a bad trend. We've called them. They've agreed to pay and have not done so."

"But we know how Gus feels about the reps, and we don't want to upset Gus Armstrong!"

"I guess we should make another call and try to get them to pay."

"I think that's a good idea. I don't want to get a call from Gus Armstrong."

"Neither do I!"

Legends and myths are untrue stories.

THE MORAL OF THIS STORY

1. Every company has its legends, myths, and stories that are untrue. This is such a legend. People believe these stories to be true and make decisions based upon them. Sometimes these decisions are bad. Be careful what you believe.

2. The rep is *not* a sacred cow. Gus Armstrong might have the final say, but you have the obligation to bring all requests to him—no matter how unfavorable they might be. The overdue accounts start at 30 days late, which might not represent a lot of money. If you believe the myth that Gus protects the reps and you wait, they'll be over 120 days late before you know it and that's a lot of money! Then it's real hard to collect or stop shipments.

3. Don't kill the messenger bringing bad news. I don't know of any messengers who brought bad news and died at my father's hands. If you want the bad news to be *heard,* be careful how you present it; speak with honesty, fairness, facts; and, provide a solution to the problem.

4. Gus Armstrong cannot read minds. Sometimes I think people feel he can read their minds. It's not fair to guess what Gus Armstrong "would have done" if you had told him. Many times he has said to me, "If they had only asked, I would have given approval. I've cut reps off who haven't paid their bills. I have fired more reps than anyone. I can't approve it if I don't know about it." Don't forget, your leaders don't read minds either. If you change the topic or the leader's name in this story, the message is still the same. Be careful what legends you believe.

87
The Big One That Got Away

Kurt Armstrong had become quite the fisherman; after all, he had been practicing off the pier in Islamorada for more than a day.

Every morning and evening Kurt would go to the pier with his rod in hand, ready to catch the "big one." He would cast his line into the water and slowly reel it in, hoping to catch the fish that would make everyone go "WOOOOW."

This was the day; Kurt just knew it. He had some special bait; steak from last night's dinner. He threw the line out and p-l-o-p went the steak into the water. Soon the line grew tight; he jerked the rod and felt the fish fight back. When the fight was over, Kurt had a Mangrove Snapper big enough to eat, but not the "big one" he had hoped for. Kurt took the fish to his mom who cleaned it and they had it for lunch.

That afternoon he played with his friends, Chris and Callie DuCoin, and his brother, Chad. It was a great vacation for Kurt, even if Dad was away on business. He had a wonderful day for shell hunting, snorkeling, and playing on the beach, but now it was time! It was time to go fishing for the "big one"—just one more time.

This time Kurt took a lawn chair and he was determined to stay on the pier until he caught the "big one." As he reached the end of the pier where many people were fishing, he set up his chair, prepared his rod and reel and threw out the line. He sat back in his chair and, being the experienced fisherman he was, slowly put his feet up on the rail. Leaning back, he gazed at the moonlight. Suddenly he felt a tug on his line. He jerked the rod and quickly began reeling faster and faster and faster; reeling just as fast as his little hand could go. He just *knew* this was it; this was the "big one." Suddenly, the end of the pole began to bend down… down… down. "I've got one; I've got one!" Kurt yelled, **"It's a big one!"** All the people fishing watched as Kurt reeled with all his might. Kurt pulled the rod up so hard that his foot came off the rail. Again, Kurt pulled the rod up and reeled, and his foot went higher! Pulling and reeling again, his foot went even higher! Suddenly he realized he had caught the shoelace on his shoe. 🔥

> *Things are not always what they seem.*
> — *Phaedrus, Roman writer*

THE MORAL OF THIS STORY

1. Be careful what you believe in. The news media covers bad news because it sells. They say, "The economy is in the worst shape since the Great Depression; unemployment is up; interest rates are high; the deficit is increasing." Leave this negative thinking at home when you come to work. Be positive, happy and proud to be an Armstronger. You have a job, better pay than most, maybe a bonus, good insurance, good working conditions, a recreation building for those long winter months, and Armstrong is growing and profitable! If anybody should be happy in this country, it should be us. So smile!

2. Be careful what you fear is real. Remember your *past* with Armstrong and become brave and wise. When you hear a rumor or fear something, ask yourself, "Have I heard this before?" Each and every year we clean and paint the building, each and every year we hear the same rumor: "They're doing this because they're going to sell the company." Things are not always what they seem.

88
E-Mail

Believe it or not, Armstrong International, Inc. now has the capability of sending e-mail (electronic messages). Yes, I know, it's the 1990s and Armstrong is just now sending e-mail. I remember seeing e-mail messages at IBM over 20 years ago. Each morning the Armstrongers come in, turn on their computers, and if there is e-mail, the computer notifies them. As they scroll through each message, they either take notes, delete the message, or hit the keyboard, returning e-mail to the original sender.

Believe it or not, I bought a computer for my home and my office which will allow me to receive faxes and e-mail. Welcome to the 20th century, David. I have used computers for many years, but never for communication, and that is my concern and the reason for this story. I have agreed to allow e-mail to be used at Armstrong International, provided the following concerns listed below in the morals are followed. E-mail has many benefits which we have all heard, but few talk about the dangers. Since we are talking about communication, they are worth mentioning. 🔥

> *Appearances are often deceiving.*
> *— Aesop's story, A Wolf In Sheep's Clothing*

The Moral Of This Story

1. The phone call, the personal visit face to face, a smiling face, the small act of giving up one's time for a personal visit, are what make people feel good. Now apply this logic not only to fellow Armstrongers, but also customers and vendors. The concern I have is people using their e-mail instead of visiting one another. People will become lazy. They will justify not having the time to make that personal visit as an excuse to send e-mail. I warn all of you that if I do not see face-to-face communication, e-mail will be **forbidden!**

2. You cannot shake hands with a keyboard. Personal contact is very important in building relationships—relationships that last. Just consider how long the custom of shaking hands has been around. It's still around because people need that human touch.

3. E-mail prevents the opportunity of talented people speaking their mind. When people brainstorm and share ideas, they are normally spontaneous. Each person feeds off the other person's comments, and together they come up with a better idea.

4. Some things never change. As when telling stories, people need to talk to each other *in person.* It creates a human bond. Don't believe me? Do you still have people who will not leave a message on your telephone answering machine at home? Why? Because they want to talk to a person, not to a machine. Do you have customers who don't like the computerized switchboards answered by a computer? Why? Because they want to talk to a human voice. What makes you think e-mail is going to replace the sound of a friendly human voice on the other end?

5. Don't let e-mail become a legend—as a great communication tool. It's not true, and never will be.

Stories about storytelling

CHAPTER XIX

89
Déjà Vu

As the week comes to an end, the busy schedule has finally opened allowing enough time to take some slides. The photographer picks up his camera and flash. While focusing the camera on the subject, the camera beeps (indicating the flash was not fully charged). The batteries need to be replaced. The photographer proceeds to the purchasing department to get more batteries.

"Excuse me," says the photographer, "I need four AAA batteries for my flash."

"I'm sorry; we don't carry batteries any more. A few years ago we found shop employees were using the batteries for their radios, so we stopped carrying them."

As she continues to explain that we can have some batteries by Monday, David Fischer interrupts, "You know, I remember reading a story once about batteries. I believe it was called 'Batteries, Batteries, Who's Got the Batteries?' (*Managing by Storying Around*, Doubleday Currency, March 1992). It had something to do with Warren Tase filling out an expense voucher because there were no batteries when he needed them. Warren charged for his mileage into town where he purchased his batteries. Warren made his point about keeping batteries at the company."

The photographer smiles at David Fischer.

She continues, "Well, you could run to the store (just down the block) and pick up some batteries."

"You don't understand," said the photographer. "I don't have time; I have to leave town in 15 minutes!"

Just then, Jerry (who was listening) stands up, grabs his coat and says, "I'll get the batteries," as he dashes out the door. A few minutes later the batteries are hand-delivered to the photographer who loads them and finally takes his slides.

Now what could be worse than writing the same story twice? You guessed it—David Armstrong in need of batteries! 🔥

> *Some stories are long forgotten; they must be retold.*

THE MORAL OF THIS STORY

1. Know our stories and you'll know our traditions, culture, future goals and vision. Simply put—you'll know what to do, what's expected of you, how to behave, what gets you promoted or fired.

2. Live each and every story. "Live" means practice what the morals say. Help others believe in the stories. Help make the stories come to life through application.

3. United we stand; divided we fall. The stories will unite us, but only if we follow them. They unite us because they speak loud and clear about what we must do as people of Armstrong.

4. Let it be known to all—we now have batteries. If you need batteries for personal use, you can now find them for sale in the cafeteria. Here's another example of creative swiping; remember the story "The Cafeteria," where the people paid for their food on the honor system? Do the same when you need batteries. This is another example of how self-management is effective in making things work more smoothly at Armstrong.

90
I'm a Seventh-grade Dropout!

_____

"**D**avid, I just entered all our new stories into our new computer. The software we bought is really nice! You won't believe all the things we can do with your stories," said Valerie Casterline, my assistant.

"Valerie, what new things can it do?"

"Well, I now have your storybook in one file which is 83 pages in length. Each time we add new stories, the software will create a new table of contents for me."

"Does it automatically reassign new page numbers?"

"Yes."

"I can also very easily download different font sizes and styles to create a nice 'desktop publishing' look. Another feature is the spelling and grammar checker. The grammar checker will even give a grade level for the document it scans. David, do you know what grade the computer gave your storybook on a 1-12th grade level?"

"No," I said, but curiosity made me ask, "What was the grade?"

"It was at a seventh-grade level."

"Seventh grade," I said, "Out of 12 grades possible? Are you sure the software is accurate? After all, I did graduate from high school!"

"Yes, I'm sure it's correct. When Dave (my husband) was editor for a newspaper in Michigan, he told me that newspapers are written at sixth-grade reading level so they're understood easily by all readers. So, don't worry, seventh-grade reading is proper for your storybook."

> *Boil it down to something I can grasp.*
> *— Max Depree*

THE MORAL OF THIS STORY

1. I'm a seventh-grade dropout... and proud of it. Remember; use simple words, simple sentences and clear thoughts to communicate effectively. Everybody should understand seventh grade reading — well, anyone who has passed the seventh grade.

2. "Newspapers are written for sixth-grade reading skills," said Val, "and they do that, David, so everybody can read the newspapers." Thanks, Val, for that trivia knowledge. Maybe it's not so trivial, particularly when writing stories or talking to your people.

3. I caught my oldest son, Chad, reading my stories. He read eight stories before I made him put the book down to eat his dinner. My youngest son, Kurt, who is nine, wanted to read the book, but I couldn't pry it from Chad's hands. Can your sons or daughters read your business reports, letters, action plans or business plans? How about your literature or advertisements?

4. The clarity with which people communicate their ideas is a good indication of the clarity of their thinking.

91
Oooops!

Upon returning to my office after a hard morning's work of MBSA (Management by Storying Around), I dreaded the pile of work which I knew would be on my desk.

As I entered my office, I noticed that a yellow message was on my phone. This was very rare since I seldom get phone messages. I take pride in that because I feel this is a true test which determines if you are a "Delegator of Authority."

On the message it said, "Please stop by and see Forrest Butterfield." I looked at the bottom of the message and saw the initials "K.L." I asked Kim Lucas if Forrest told her why he was calling me.

"He didn't tell me, David. I'm sorry." I stuffed the message in my pocket and went about my work.

Later that day, I found myself near Forrest's office and decided to drop in. He was in his office sitting at his desk.

"Forest, I understand you want to see me about something."

"Yes, I would like to show you some of the prototypes I did several years ago for the WT Trap. As you're aware, this design was later developed into the Silver Nugget and MT-1 Trap. Recently, it became clear to me that very few people knew I was involved in the original design of the Silver Nugget. I thought you would be interested in hearing the story behind the story."

Immediately, I remembered writing a story about our Silver Nuggets (see story "Silver Nuggets") and the champions that made it possible. I also remembered that we failed to mention Forrest's name. Forrest obviously had a lot of pride in his earlier work and, since the product was very successful, wanted to be recognized for his contributions.

"Forrest, I never heard that you were involved in the original design of the Silver Nugget, or if I was made aware, I simply forgot to mention it in the story. I can see by these prototypes and the sequence of events on how the product was developed that you were definitely involved in the Silver Nugget. I'm glad you took it upon yourself to make sure I knew the whole story. Thank you for all your fine work."

"That's all I really wanted, David. I just wanted someone to say 'thank you' or give me a handshake. I don't want to cause any problems or make you think that I'm upset about your story."

"I understand, Forrest. I'm glad you brought this to my attention."

Later that day, I went back to Forrest's office and presented him with a plaque for our recognition program. The plaque said "Success" and I added a written commentary to our newsletter describing Forrest's contribution. Oh! He also got a story. 🔥

> *Stories have purpose only if read or heard.*
> *Don't keep them to yourself.*

THE MORAL OF THIS STORY

1. Does Managing by Storying Around really work? You know it does when someone brings a mistake to your attention. First they had to read the story to find the mistake; second, they had to really care before they would bring it to your attention.

2. Storytelling has risks associated with it—so does any recognition program. If we let these fears prevent us from implementing recognition programs, we lose a valuable tool in leadership.

Recognition is needed so that when people do something right, they can feel good about it. A story also lets others know what we cherish as good business behavior.

3. The fear of failure is worse than failure itself. If you decide to use stories in your leadership style, you *will* make mistakes. My fear that one day somebody would rake me over the coals for failing to tell the whole story has never come true.

92
The Library
Checkout Card

Every six months, Armstrong International, Inc. prints a new book full of stories. It's not an expensive book, yet it's attractive. With the Armstrong logo embossed in gold on its white cover and the black spiral bound on its side, the book is quite appealing. On the inside there is an introduction, a table of contents and all the stories divided by chapters. The page numbers are marked with different sized print and bold print is used in the morals. We did, however, have to purchase a new laser printer and computer with software that editors use in the publishing business.

We send these books to our divisions every six months. Each Armstrong division has an "ambassador" who collects the storybooks and distributes them throughout the plant so people can read them. Every time we send out the new storybooks, we have the ambassadors return the old books. We do this to find out if people are reading the books and to make sure the books are in the proper locations. Using a white cover shows dirty finger prints, so at a glance you can tell if the book has been read.

Warrick Controls once returned their books with a surprise inside. As we opened one book, we found a white envelope taped to the inside cover with a white card inside. At the top of the card it said *Managing by Storying Around* by David Armstrong. It was obvious this was used as a "library checkout card" in case someone wanted to take the book home. This was given to the ambassador at Warrick and the person's name was checked off when they returned the book (similar to what you would find when checking out a library book).

We copied this idea and passed it along to the other divisions.

> *You know your stories are popular when you need a "library checkout card" to keep track of your storybook.*

THE MORAL OF THIS STORY

1. Stories must be easy to find. In previous stories you've heard me talk about printing stories and posting them on bulletin boards for everyone to see. By distributing these storybooks to our divisions every six months and placing them in key locations our stories become more popular. Our problem has been that people walk off with the storybooks; therefore, other employees no longer have access to them. Using the "library checkout card" can solve this problem and still let the people take the book home.

2. Storybooks are free to Armstrong people. If an employee wants a storybook, we are more than happy to give it to them. The story ambassador simply reorders another storybook from Armstrong. Normally, the books end up missing because sales-men and our partners take copies when they see them in the lobby. Special visitors have also been known to take a copy with them.

3. Sometimes we are too close to the forest to see the trees. It took Warrick Controls to remind us we needed a "library check-out card" to help track our books. Thanks to Warrick, we now have a better system of sharing the books with our employees, thus maintaining our readership.

93
The Ten Commandments

Long, long ago, there was a wise man named Moses. One day Moses climbed a mountain called Mount Sinai. When he reached the top, he was on holy ground and God spoke to him giving him ten commandments people must follow:

 I. You shall have no other Gods before me.
 II. You shall not make for yourself a graven image.
 III. You shall not take the name of the Lord your God in vain.
 IV. Keep the Sabbath Day holy.
 V. Honor your father and mother.
 VI. You shall not kill.
 VII. Neither shall you commit adultery.
 VIII. Neither shall you steal.
 IX. Neither shall you bare false witness against your neighbor.
 X. Neither shall you covet your neighbor's wife, house, fields, or anything that's your neighbor's.

These commandments were cast in two stone tablets.

> *Good stories are worth much;*
> *good stories retold are worth much more.*

THE MORAL OF THIS STORY

1. It is crucial to retell a story to keep it alive. You see, physical objects like the stone tablets can last for many, many years. But the stories which stand behind them and breathe life into them, *always* stand just one generation from extinction. This is a story about religion. We also have many stories about our company that must be *retold*.

2. It is not the object or events that we pass on to our children, but it's a story that is our heritage. Without the story of Moses climbing Mount Sinai and God writing the ten commandments on stone tablets, the tablets become just stone. The same is true for Armstrong. It becomes a pile of bricks. The story about why plant three was built in its location is lost—unless you read the story titled, "Our Promise to Fred Kemp," *Managing by Storying Around*, Doubleday Currency, March 1992.

3. Make no mistake... remove the story from the event or object and it loses its significance. Each generation must be told the story as accurately and as often as possible, or the next generation will say, "There was once a man named Moses who climbed a mountain—I can't remember the name of the mountain—and God gave him the ten commandments on stone tablets. The ten commandments said:

    I. You shall have no other Gods before me.
    II. You shall not make for yourself a graven image.
    III. You shall not take the name of the Lord your God in vain.
    IV. Keep the Sabbath Day holy.
    V. Honor your father and mother.
    VI. You shall not kill.
    VII. Neither shall you commit adultery.
    VIII. Neither shall you steal.
    IX. Neither shall you bare false witness against your neighbor.
    X. Neither shall you covet your neighbor's wife, house, fields, or anything that's your neighbor's.

The next generation will tell the story, "There was once a man named Moses who climbed a mountain—I can't remember the name of the mountain—and God gave him the ten commandments on stone tablets, but I can't remember what they said. By the third or fourth generation, the story will go, "There once was a man—I can't remember his name—who climbed a mountain and he received some stone tablets with commandments on them from God. I can't remember what God said or how many commandments there were, but I hope the story will help us keep our faith." Now do you see why stories about our company must be retold faithfully? If not, we forget important details in the stories, such as the name of Moses, the mountain or even the Ten Commandments. Did you remember all Ten Commandments?

94
The Wizard

This is a story about a wizard, so named because he invented more products than anyone in his time. The wizard had just finished his latest invention—a phonograph. The unit had a crank which was turned to generate the power, and a large wooden funnel that projected sound. Sounds (usually music) were recorded on cylinders.

Thomas Edison soon began to focus on his many other projects which were in the early stages of development. Shortly thereafter, Alexander Graham Bell made an announcement: "A new and improved phonograph is available from the Bell Company." It was reported to be much better than the Edison phonograph.

Edison quickly called a press conference (with a unit in-hand) and revealed: "I hold a phonograph which will be available for purchase very soon. It is *better* than the Bell unit." Due to Edison's reputation, most financial backers supported his unit versus Bell's.

The surprising end to this story is that, Edison, in fact, *did not* have a new unit. He was actually holding an old unit. But due to his reputation as "the wizard" he was able to bluff and gain the financial support which Alexander Graham Bell needed. Of course, shortly thereafter, he did produce a better phonograph—living up to his solid reputation. 🔥

An Oldie, But Goody

THE MORAL OF THIS STORY

1. Be selective on the stories you tell, if you feel you don't have time to tell stories. Pick stories from the best minds of our time. Successful people, such as Edison, normally have wonderful stories—stories you may never hear from anyone else. Their stories of success are timeless.

2. Edison was famous for his stories. Some were tales, some were myths, but many had the ring of truth to them. The stories he told established his reputation as "the wizard." Yes, it can be said that his many inventions also helped his reputation, but telling stories made his reputation bigger than life.

3. Edison told many, many stories to establish his reputation. Here's a man who believed in my teachings about storytelling. Stories can create the atmosphere you wish to have within your company. Remember, to build a personal reputation or a corporate atmosphere, stories must be told often—to the point where they become traditional, or commonplace in your company.

4. "I cannot tell a lie; I chopped down the cherry tree," said George Washington. Did this really happen? It doesn't matter. What matters is telling the story over and over and over, to the point where it has become part of our national mythology. Becoming one of our nation's best-known myths is not based on the story being true, but on its being repeated to each generation. Don't forget to repeat the moral if you want it known as well. Remember, the moral to Washington's story was "honesty is the best policy."

95
Another Wizard

"**F**ollow the yellow brick road; follow the yellow brick road; follow, follow, follow, follow, follow the yellow brick road. We're off to see the wizard, the Wonderful Wizard of Oz."

As the song continues, Dorothy, the tin man and the lion dance down the yellow brick road. Soon they are confronted by the Wicked Witch of the West who wants Dorothy's red ruby shoes. Dorothy took the shoes from the wicked witch's sister—the Wicked Witch of the East.

Dorothy finally reaches the Wizard of Oz, who, at the end of the story, offers to take Dorothy and her dog, Fido, back to Kansas in his airplane.

> *"There's no place like home."*

THE MORAL OF THIS STORY

1. Our society and businesses have their favorite stories. Neither needs to finish their stories; they've been heard so many times the endings are known. When you heard "follow the yellow brick road," you immediately knew this was the story about the Wizard of Oz. You even knew how the story ended without my finishing it. I've already told you Armstrong's favorite stories: "The Cafeteria," "The Production Bonus" and "The Blue Tag Special."

2. "There's no place like home." This is the moral behind *The Wizard of Oz*, where at the end of Dorothy's dream she awakes repeating, "There's no place like home; there's no place like home." Familiar stories always have a moral. Normally, the moral is very powerful. "The Blue Tag Special" is about quality where each employee checks their own quality. Believe me — our people know this moral and live it!

3. How do you spot a familiar story? You normally hear it repeated many times. Familiar stories are often told to new employees before any other stories. The final test is when you know most of the details in the story. You probably knew the scarecrow was the fourth person dancing down the yellow brick road, or that a hot air balloon was how Dorothy got home, not in an airplane. Finally, the dog was not Fido, it was Toto.

96
Your Name is Worth Money

It was Thursday afternoon when Ken Clay, financial controller, approached Mike Fury in the assembly department, "Here you go Mike. I'm sure you can find a good use for this."

"Thanks, Ken, I sure can. Wait a minute, you gave me two checks."

"That's right, don't you remember? This week we pay the production bonus?"

"Oh, that's right, this bonus should be great since it was at $3 per hour." says Mike (see "Production Bonus" in *Managing by Storying Around*, Doubleday Currency, March 1992).

Mike heads over to the desk of Bill McClane, foreman, sits down and endorses his name on the back of the checks. Just as he finishes, he hears,

"Hey, Mike, can you come over and help lift this?"

Mike puts his pen down, "Sure, I'll be right there."

Later that night, Jim Pisco, one of the men who cleans the shop at night and works for an outside contractor, Herb Abrams, notices two paychecks on the desk. He picks them up and realizes they have been endorsed. Knowing they can be cashed, he immediately takes them to Dick Hay, quality insurance inspector for the night crew.

"Dick," Jim says, "I found these paychecks in the humidifier department and they've been endorsed. Would you make sure that Mike gets them? I am sure he's worried—they're worth a lot of money."

"Thanks, Jim, I'll be happy to make sure Mike gets them."

Dick folds the checks and puts them in an envelope.

The next morning, Mike, in a panic, is looking for his paychecks. He thinks to himself, "Where did I leave them? I hope nobody cashed them!"

Shortly thereafter, he receives an envelope with his two checks and a note from Dick Hay explaining the story.

> *Hearing a story can be the next best thing to being there.*

THE MORAL OF THIS STORY

1. Storytelling is gaining popularity. Dick Hay and others at Armstrong International, Inc., Michigan are starting to tell stories. They see the positive effect it has and its simplicity.

2. Storytelling is more instinctive than something you learn. Telling stories is simple. We do it almost without thought. To become master storytellers, our stories must have enticing titles, we must practice telling them, and our stories should have good morals.

3. Stories can be told by anybody, at any place, at any time. Dick Hay stopped me in the aisle of the manufacturing plant (any place). He caught me at 5:30 p.m. (any time) and told me this story. Since I started telling stories, I have found that our people tell stories all the time.

4. Storytelling needs a star and Jim Pisco is that star. For stories to be told it helps to have a heroic deed performed by a heroic person. Jim has debts to pay like everyone else. He did not give in to greed as tempting as it was. He must have read my story titled, "Lead Us Not Into Temptation." Remember, he could have cashed those checks because they were endorsed.

97
A Story from the Past

The following photograph of Adam E. Armstrong, founder of Armstrong Machine Works, was taken by Lawrence F. Armstrong (Adam's son), and it's a **SWELL SHOT— A TOP PIX**—or, as Lew Sandberg would say:

"A LOOZY!"

Paul Lizst Ulrich, chief engineer at Armstrong International, Inc., Michigan, told a story about a glib salesman who tried to sell Adam a battery of automatic machines which would do certain operations faster, and supplant maybe a dozen men! All Adam said was, "No, I guess not, the work is being done fast enough, and the men would only have to go out and look for new jobs!"

Tom Rea, sales manager, said in 1928, "When the new Armstrong building was constructed, another salesman suggested factory-rib window glass. This would let in all the light," he said, "but the employees couldn't see out, so their attention couldn't be distracted from their work!" To this salesman, Adam answered, "No, I guess not, I'm not building a prison!" 🔥

I never knew the powers of a story until I heard one told.

THE MORAL OF THIS STORY

1. These stories—from Tom and Paul—couldn't be forgotten.
A good story is passed on from generation to generation. What makes a good story? A reader enjoys a story that involves them personally. That only happens when the story is familiar. If you have something in common with the story you can feel its message.

2. The phrases "a loozy," "a top pix," and "glib salesman" have changed, but not the point of the story. Stories don't become outdated because *old* slang has changed. The moral of this story is timely even if the names in the story are long past. Other details in this story, such as quotes from Adam, keep the story alive throughout the decades.

3. Stories help give a snapshot of Armstrong's secret to success— better than any balance sheet, profit and loss statement, business plan, action plan, audit or customer survey.

4. A company is the shadow of the man, *and the people*, who create it—out of TRUST, TRUTH, FAIRNESS, INTELLIGENCE and UNDERSTANDING.

Adam E. Armstrong

98
How to Write or Tell a Story

Below is a detailed checklist which I use to write my stories. I hope you find this helpful when writing your stories.

How I Write The Story:

1. Find a heroic deed performed by a heroic person.
2. List *factual* information. Your stories should be true to hold meaning.
3. Use a catchy title to capture the interest of the reader.
4. Include several paragraphs (The Moral Of This Story) which summarize the story. Emphasize those principles you want practiced within your company.
5. Focus on one central theme in the summary, such as innovation, or customers, or vision, or quality, etc.
6. Verify all facts with persons in story.
7. Keep each story one page in length.
8. People like to see their names in print. Use their names in your story.
9. Use words that build mental images, so that readers can visualize characters and situations.
10. Use simple words, sixth- or seventh-grade reading level.
11. Use dialogue to create the feeling of a story.
12. Capitalize and use bold print on the first letter of the first word.
13. Use titles and company name.

14. Small paragraphs are better.
15. Fewer words are better than more words.
16. Quote yourself or someone famous.
17. Bold print the first line of each moral to summarize the moral.
18. Date your story.
19. Don't forget your copyright!

Implementation Of Storytelling:

1. I tell the stories whenever I want to make a point or coach someone.
2. We post the stories on bulletin boards throughout our companies. This allows factory and office personnel to learn who the people are in a sister division, what the company sells, and the kind of behavior we expect from our employees.
3. I hand deliver the story, in a wooden frame, to the person who the story is written about. I always hand-write a *personal* comment with my signature at the top right-hand corner.
4. The stories are used to train current and new employees.
5. We have produced slides of some stories for presentations at large meetings.
6. Note pads made by our printing department show story titles in the upper left-hand corner in a bright shaded box. Below the shaded box, we show the quote or moral found in that story. Every time someone makes a note, they are reminded of our stories and their morals or quote.

Potential Problems:

1. Finding heroic stories is time-consuming and difficult.
2. Sometimes you forget the name of a person who was part of the story, causing hurt feelings.
3. Printing the correct person's name (who the story is really about) can be difficult. Everybody seems to believe they are the person who made the story possible and they should be identified. Perception is a difficult thing to deal with (fortunately, it only happens on rare occasions).
4. You will never get the story 100 percent accurate. This is only a problem in *your* mind.
5. Don't worry about missing a moral—you want the reader or listener to think of morals.

Benefits From Storytelling:

1. Recognition of heroic people.
2. Tells your people how you want them to behave.
3. Makes events more memorable.
4. Promotes the *soft* stuff which is difficult to do. Real personal stories help.
5. Maintains a friendly family atmosphere within the company.
6. Supports, spreads and explains the company's culture.
7. Forces your leaders to go out and find stories—which gets them involved with people in all areas of the company (Managing by Storying Around—MBSA).
8. Provides training to new and current employees.
9. Unites the employees to follow one vision, one set of core values, one set of traditions.
10. Promotes tradition and culture.
11. Helps "break the ice" with new employees.

99
Writer's Block

In the corner sits a wastebasket. Flowing over its rim are little white balls of paper. Some are falling onto the floor.

R...I...P...

Another piece of paper is pulled from the typewriter, wadded up in frustration and thrown at the wastebasket; it lands on the floor next to the other white balls.

Another piece of clean white paper is rolled into the typewriter. The author ponders, trying to think of another story. We've all seen this on television or in the movies, but we've never *really* experienced it.

Being a disciple of storytelling, you will one day find yourself frustrated while trying to write or tell a story. Here are some helpful hints to help you through those troublesome times. 🔥

> *Where there are no stories, the people perish.*

THE MORAL OF THIS STORY

1. How to get in the mood of storytelling? You will find some places are easier for writing and thinking of a story. How do you find this special place? Start writing stories in different places and you will see a pattern—a place where you finish the most stories. I like creating my stories in the car while driving to the airport.

2. When and what do you write about? If you know what to look for, stories are easier to find. If I want to write stories about tradition, I talk to retirees or older employees in our company, who have several stories to tell. Just make a list of 20 to 50 topics you want to discuss and go where the people *familiar* with them can be found.

3. *Where* do your stories come from? After my first 30 stories, I began to focus on those Armstrong International, Inc. *divisions* I had not written about. This led me to visit those divisions, where I found more stories. If your company is smaller or your responsibilities are not company-wide, think about departments.

4. *Who* are your stories about? After my first 60 stories I began to look at those *individuals* I had not written about. I began visiting and talking to them. Guess what? I found more stories. Once again, becoming more focused on a topic, whether it be a location or person helps prevent writer's block.

5. No story is perfect. Don't rewrite the story. We all take pride in our work and our natural tendency is to be a perfectionist. Get it down on paper, put it away for a few days and look at it again. You'll be amazed; suddenly, the story appears!

6. Practice, practice, practice. Just like a professional athlete, the more you practice, the better storyteller you will become.

Rookie
storytellers

CHAPTER XX

100
The Story of
Vittorio Russo

Dedicated to Dr. Demarteau and Father Jeammart

Back in 1984, Vittorio was a student in a technical school of the Liège area. When he was hired by Armstrong he was under 18 years old and the compulsory schooling in Belgium is 18. However, this was done in full agreement with his school manager, who told me he would much prefer to know that Vittorio was working at Armstrong rather than running over the streets with his motorbike. In fact, he didn't show up much at school. Well, he kept working with us until his departure for the army service time.

After his service time, while he was looking for a job, he was quite lucky, since we needed some help in our machine shop department. I knew he had no certification but he had enough basic experience, bearing in mind safety, when working with machines. After a certain time, however, he developed some kind of allergy, which finally turned into a severe eczema, when working in contact with oil or fluid coolant. Even handling parts, which had been in contact with those products, was enough to hurt him so badly that he couldn't work for weeks.

What to do? We tried to find some special work for Vittorio but as soon as he was touching some products his skin reacted quite immediately. No medical treatment helped him and during one talk with the doctor, who was in charge of the medical control of our shop employees (this is required by law), we came to the conclusion that Vittorio had no chance to continue that way. The only solution was to dismiss him and let the social security take care of him, in case he couldn't find another job.

We found one more possibility: welding the buckets for our stainless steel traps. Stainless steel is one clean product but the material is very thin and does require some dexterity curing TIG welding. We knew this and Vittoria had no experience in welding! Training people has always been one of our challenges in our Belgian factory. The results were surprising: Vittorio learned extremely fast and very shortly, he was capable to produce quality products with the highest efficiency. Today he is still our bucket welder and has totally overcome his skin problems. He has a nice family with two children and purchased his house some time ago. I am proud to say that Armstrong has contributed to this success.

Necessity is the mother of invention.
— *Latin Proverb*

THE MORAL OF THIS STORY

1. Vittorio's case is not the only one in our Herstal plant. By proper training, we have allowed other people to promote themselves and be proud of being part of our family. Despite the fact they didn't have the necessary qualifications, those people, however, all had one common quality: they badly wanted to learn and to work.

2. You can't find skilled labor? The greatest potential is inside your company.

3. We think we are promoting jobs! In fact, in Belgium we are killing work with our Union's rules and government laws.

Authored by:
Roger Closset, General Manager-1995
Armstrong International, Belgium
and David M. Armstrong

101
The Long... Too Long
Packing Table

I always have been proud of my factory layout In Herstal, Belgium. Over the years, when product lines changed, or when new machines had to be installed, I always thought I did the best to use with efficiency the space available and provide people with the most convenient and safe work environments.

One day, however, I will always remember. It was on a Friday after the day work when Roger Feyth, working in our shipping department, came to my office and asked me whether I would be interested in one major improvement of the shipping area. Of course, I was! This area always had been crowded around the packing table (five meters long) required for packing our humidifier's steam dispersion manifolds.

Roger started to explain his ideas about the reorganization but because of the many changes he was suggesting, I got confused and asked him if he could put these on paper. The next Monday, Roger presented the sketches he made over the weekend roughly on school pads. Immediately I realized the benefit of the project but on the other hand I also realized that not only the shipping area (his department) was affected by the move, but also others such as humidifier assembly and the stainless steel trap line.

I got enthusiastic about the idea and asked Roger to be responsible of the project. I required, however, that he discuss this project with all the people concerned and get all the assistance needed. Last, but not least, the work should not be carried out during busy working days. The work was carried out one weekend with one team working under Roger's supervision, using the sketches he made. Today, if you visit our factory, you would hardly imagine this long... too long packing table was ever here. Of course, our shipping department is still very crowded today, even more than before. This is because Armstrong International in Herstal, Belgium, is servicing not only all European countries, West and East, but also the USA and some other countries.

Since other people came up with ideas we have proceeded with other moves, which helped to maintain the highest efficiency in our shop. I sincerely do hope that many more will come.

The most unused factory asset is the human imagination.

THE MORAL OF THIS STORY

1. Even when things are working fine, there are always possibilities to improve.

2. People performing the work sometimes know best. Others may think they know best all the time, but that is not true.

3. Listen to your people. If you won't, why are they working for you?

4. Be ready to accept changes... even if ideas are not necessarily coming from supervisors or middle management.

Authored by:
Roger Closset, General Manager-1995
Armstrong International, Inc., Belgium
and David M. Armstrong

102
Armstrong's Guard Tower

The letter read,

My dear, young friend, David:

Grandma Annie Grover (your grandmother) loaned me her book that you wrote. I read it with rapt attention, being acquainted with many of the principal characters. First of all, I would like to say, my 35 years of experience working for Armstrong International, Inc., Michigan has been an enjoyable experience. My oldest son, Dick, worked during his college days; Judy during nurses training; and now, Dan and Steve, for which I am thankful. Here's a little story which is true:

When Plant II was built, the shop office was put on the second floor over the washroom. It seems there were a few who said they felt like they were in a prison with a guard tower in the center. The office was removed and sometime later converted to an inspection department. When Plant III was built, management remembered what the people had said and built the washroom upstairs and the office downstairs. I wonder how many companies would have listened to such a complaint?

Sincerely,

Richard Torrans

Behind every great company are great stories.

THE MORAL OF THIS STORY

1. Even retirees tell stories. Richard Torrans retired in 1987. Many of our retirees have stories which are long forgotten. They must be retold. Their stories are not outdated. The action Armstrong took in changing the location of the office because people felt it was a guard tower shows that Armstrong cares about its people. Today the popular style of leadership is to care about people and treat them with respect. In the past, leaders were not as interested in their employees' feelings, yet, even before it became popular, Armstrong still cared for its people. But then you wouldn't know this if a retiree hadn't told his story.

2. Only stories last forever! Dick Torrans may be retired, but his story lives on. Stories can live many generations, but only if told. Stories will be around long after people are gone, machinery is replaced, literature is changed, products become obsolete; the only way stories die is when they are not retold.

3. Stories make events more memorable. The washroom and office are just brick and mortar until Dick's story is told. This story brings the washroom to life.

103
Growing Somewhere?

My name is Joe Moran and I am a fan of people who are motivated, looking for change, and are constantly growing. I enjoy stories that point you in the right direction. I believe in all of this and want to keep practicing it all. I've been looking for a place where all this happens.

It's a place that people are proud to be a part of. A place where people are happy to come to: They look forward to it. A place people say and yell, "hello" to each other. A place people call in sick only when they are sick. A place people would choose to work for a lifetime. A place where people are happy. A place where people call home. I have found this place, have you? 🔥

> *Growing places are the only places going places.*

THE MORAL TO THIS STORY

1. Are you a part of a place like I just mentioned? If the answer is no, find it or create it. The best places help you while you help them.

2. Are you growing and learning? If not, are you in the right place? Good companies are constantly training and developing as times change.

3. Are you happy with where you are going? If so, help someone else do the same. If not, find someone who is and ask them how they got there.

Authored by:
Joe Moran, Purchasing/Production Manager
Armstrong-Yoshitake, Michigan
and David M. Armstrong

P.S.   This story was handed to me during an interview with Joe Moran. After a series of interviews, Joe was hired to work at Armstrong-Yoshitake. This story shows that Joe believes in Armstrong's culture.

104
The Fund's Most Wanted

Data alert! It was approximately 6:30 p.m. on a Thursday evening when she received the call. The voice at the other end said, "One of your customers just called and said his data is not in its correct format. According to him it's missing information."

There was a pause. "Who is the customer and what seems to be the problem?" questioned the voice on the other end.

The caller was Mark Crum (computer room operator) in the computer room, and the voice at the other end was Debbie Lyons, data marketing services coordinator. Upon hearing the disturbing news, Debbie promptly called the customer—from her home.

"What seems to be the problem with your tape?" Debbie asked the customer.

"Well, I only have about 500 records on my tape and I should have several thousand," answered the customer.

Debbie assured the customer she would look into the problem and immediately get back with him. After hanging up with the customer, Debbie promptly called Mark back. He in turn conferenced in Les Sormberger (manager of the computer room). The trio talked of the dilemma and determined that all Special Data Product customers were affected by the glitch. A decision was immediately made to re-run all the magnetic tapes, and to send them overnight via Federal Express. Mark quickly started the processing again, and new sets of tapes were promptly delivered to our customers.

Before any of the customers affected by the data error received their defective tape, we called to inform them that a replacement marked "correct version" would arrive in the morning.

"I wanted you to be aware that the original tape you will receive this morning has incomplete data. You will also receive a tape tagged "corrected version" which has all the complete data," Debbie informed each of the customers affected.

It is important to note that the primary reason we found out so quickly that we had a problem with the tape run, was due to the fact that the customer who discovered the missing data picks his tape up directly from our office every Thursday afternoon (and processes it immediately). Debbie mails out all the other tapes via overnight delivery each Thursday morning. Thus, the majority of our customers receive their information Friday morning.

We could have been faced with a potential disaster on Friday. However, due to the quick action of Mark, Debbie and Les, were able to turn a potential negative situation into a positive one. They also understood that we were darned serious about taking care of them! This was clearly evidenced in the way Debbie, Mark and Les handled the situation.

Upon review of data, Beth Clatworthy, the computer programmer, found the glitch in the original tape. After consulting with Laura Hooks, the programmer/analyst, the pair went through the necessary steps to avert any further data problems. Again, our customers realized that we take them very seriously.

Some people may think you can't measure customer service excellence — that it's a "soft" intangible thing. They are right, you know. Without the excellent customer service exhibited by the five people noted in this story, we would have nothing to measure, because we would have no customers. 🔥

THE MORAL OF THIS STORY

1. The true sense of urgency exhibited by Debbie, Mark and Les averted a potential disaster. Many special Data Product customers have strict deadlines to meet when processing their data. A prolonged delay can affect their overall production process.

2. By detecting the cause of the glitch, the same problem will be avoided in the future. Beth and Laura made absolutely certain that this glitch was eliminated by programming a "check" into the system which will essentially search for errors of this sort in the future. This will ultimately rid the program of any possible future data discrepancies.

3. Turn a potential negative into a positive experience for both you and your customers. We all encounter a crisis at one time or another. The important thing is how well we handle these situations when they arise. By attacking the problem immediately, we all become winners. Our customers understood that we had a problem. But instead of making it their problem, we made it ours. Because of the prompt and honest response our customers received, they recognized our hustle and desire to service their needs accurately and timely.

Authored by:
David Casterline, Demand Manager
Armstrong Machine Works
and David M. Armstrong

105
Coming To America

This wonderful story begins with my first overseas visit in 1967, at a very impressionable age and very interested in the big, wide world, I visited two companies, both of which I had communicated with before and from whom we had been importing equipment.

At the first company, I was very warmly welcomed by the sales director, who was interested to meet a customer from one of the old colonial countries. After a very scrumptious lunch together with his fellow directors, I startled the company by requesting that, if possible, I would like to look around the factory floor and view the products that we were importing and particularly how they were being made.

This request led to some concern—and after having been handed down some three times, I was shown around by the shop steward. My personal opinion was that the directors had very little, if any, direct communication with those that did the work.

The second company was a totally different experience. I was shown around personally by the company president, who knew everyone on the shop floor and even stopped at the floor cleaner and complimented him on his son's fine performance in the previous evening's game of ball.

What a difference between the companies as far as the impression that was left with myself, the customer. The second company gave me confidence that management and people worked efficiently and happily toward a common goal, and the other was one of a total void between the two, to the detriment of the product.

It was some time ago, but if my memory serves me correctly, the president of the second company responded to the name of "Gus Armstrong."

Authored by:
Rod Mountain, President & Owner
Armstrong Steam Ltd., Edenvale, South Africa
and David M. Armstrong

TO BE CONTINUED...